WANTING TO BE HER

TO BE HER

Body Image Secrets

Victoria Won't Tell You

Michelle Graham

InterVarsity Press
Downers Grove, Illinois

InterVarsity Press
P.O. Box 1400, Downers Grove, IL 60515 1426
World Wide Web: www.ivpress.com
E-mail: mail@ivpress.com

InterVarsity Press® is the book-publishing division of InterVarsity Christian Fellowship/USA®, a student movement active on campus at hundreds of universities, colleges and schools of nursing in the United States of America, and a member movement of the International Fellowship of Evangelical Students. For information about local and regional activities, write Public Relations Dept., InterVarsity Christian Fellowship/USA, 6400 Schroeder Rd., P.O. Box 7895, Madison, WI 53707-7895, or visit the IVCF website at <www.intervarsity.org>.

All Scripture quotations, unless otherwise indicated, are taken from the Holy Bible, New International Version®. NIV®. *Copyright ©1973, 1978, 1984 by International Bible Society. Used by permission of Zondervan Publishing House. All rights reserved.*

The stories in this book are based on the author's experiences and interviews with individuals. Names and identifying details have been changed to protect the privacy of the individuals involved.

Design: Cindy Kiple

Images: Model being photographed: Willie Maldonado/Getty Images
 Woman with clipboard: Chabruken/Getty Images

ISBN 0-8308-3266-1

Printed in the United States of America ∞

Library of Congress Cataloging-in-Publication Data

Graham, Michelle, 1971-
 Wanting to be her: body image secrets Victoria won't tell you /
 Michelle Graham.
   p. cm.
 Includes bibliographical references (p.   )
 ISBN 0-8308-3266-1 (pbk.: alk. paper)
 1. Christian women—Religious life. 2. Body image in
 women—Religious aspects—Christianity. 3. Self-acceptance in
 women—Religious aspects—Christianity. I. Title.

 BV4527.G69 2005
 248.8'43—dc22

2004029590

| P | 18 | 17 | 16 | 15 | 14 | 13 | 12 | 11 | 10 | 9 | 8 | 7 | 6 | 5 |
| Y | 17 | 16 | 15 | 14 | 13 | 12 | 11 | 10 | 09 | 08 | 07 | 06 | | |

To my children . . .

may you grow to know how beautiful God made you.

And to Byron . . .

who reminds me daily how much

I am loved by my Maker.

❧ CONTENTS

✍ ACKNOWLEDGMENTS

*T*hank you . . .

To the women who were willing to bare their souls with me about body image.

To those who encouraged a first-time writer to write: Phyllis Le Peau, Greg Jao, Byron Graham, Andy Le Peau and Cindy Bunch.

To the students and staff of InterVarsity who have helped me walk my journey with Jesus. Especially to the students of Northern Illinois University, who consistently encourage me with their deep hunger for God and their zeal to serve him.

To Mom and Dad, who have modeled God's unconditional love to me. And for dad's tips and tidbits. Maybe your years as an English teacher and your love for good writing actually rubbed off a bit.

And to my husband, Byron, whose affirmation of women's gifts and whose love for me resulted in self-sacrifice so that I could have writing time. I love you.

1 ✐ THE LIE WE BUY

Beauty and Culture

THE THREE WISHES OF EVERY MAN:

TO BE HEALTHY, TO BE RICH BY

HONEST MEANS, AND TO BE BEAUTIFUL.

✐ *Plato*

*N*ostalgia. Walks down memory lane fill me with warm fuzz-ies—right up there with a warm bubble bath and a good cup of café mocha. When I think about my childhood, I have an index of "re-member when" images that rank high on the list. The treehouse my dad built, learning to bake pumpkin seeds, *Highlights* magazine, paja-mas with footies, candy necklaces and my Easy Bake Oven. But there is no memory that stands out more than my obsession with Barbie.

My sister and I owned an enormous collection of Barbie parapher-nalia. In addition to our Barbie dolls, we had the Barbie truck, the Barbie Corvette, the Barbie motor home and the Barbie mansion, complete with Barbie furniture right down to the Barbie coffee table and the Barbie silverware in the kitchen. Our Barbies had an abun-dant wardrobe of the latest fashions, and most of Barbie's time was spent changing in and out of her very cool clothes. Of course we also had Ken and a knockoff version called the Sunshine Family, but they all took a backseat to the star of the show.

There was one problem. My Barbie had come with curly hair. Very early on I put her hair in a ponytail with a rubber band, and I left it that way too long in Barbie years. When I finally took the rubber band out, the plastic hair had become so tangled that it stuck straight up on the top of her head—even Don King would have been embarrassed. There she was, doomed to a life of bad hair days.

My sister, on the other hand, owned Malibu Barbie. Her selling point had been a perfect tan and long beautiful hair. I was so jealous. I secretly coveted her golden locks on behalf of my Barbie. Some days I even suggested that we switch Barbies, but my sister never showed any interest. I think she was on to me.

A BARBIE WORLDVIEW

Thinking about it now, I can almost taste the irony. A Barbie with flaws. Isn't Barbie supposed to be the ideal role model for little girls? At least that's what her website claims. Barbie is supposed to inspire. She's been a cheerleader, a college student, a power executive, an astronaut, even an athlete in the WNBA. There is nothing she doesn't own—cars, houses, clothes, boats, swimming pools, even her own McDonald's franchise. She has never known failure. She has never been without a boyfriend. She has never needed plastic surgery. Or has she?

Barbie was born in 1959, when Mattel cofounder Ruth Handler approached her all-male design staff with the idea of a three-dimensional doll to replace the paper-doll fad. The result was a fashion doll that became a cultural icon of the ideal beautiful woman—tall, slender, curvy and white. But if Barbie were a real human being, she would need some major reconstructive surgery just to survive. It's been estimated that if Barbie had an average bust size of 36 inches, her proportions would make her anywhere from 6 feet 2 inches to 7 feet 5 inches tall. No wonder she was able to play for the WNBA. In order to achieve her hourglass figure, she would need to have two ribs removed along with several major organs. Barbie has no hormonal cycle to affect her complexion and no metabolism to struggle with. And if you ask me, that gap between her thighs could only be the result of a major bone deformity in her hips. What began as a fantasy of perfect beauty actually turned out to be a freak.

This is the image that has been marketed to young girls all over the world as an inspiration to womanhood. And we eat it up. Barbie has become a $1.5 billion-a-year industry. "Barbie touches so many aspects of a girl's psyche, from adventure to independence to dreams of aspirations, that the emotional connections with the Barbie brand run deep."

Don't worry, I'm not on a Barbie-burning crusade. And I'm certainly no expert on the psychological effects of Barbie on young children. But I do know that at a very young age I bought into the idea that unless my Barbie was physically perfect, she wasn't as good as the other Barbies on the block. In fact, she embarrassed me.

There's nothing quite like a glance at a Victoria's Secret catalog to invoke a flood of insecurities and feelings of disappointment.

As I grew into adulthood, I left my Barbie behind. Unfortunately I continued my Barbie philosophy of life. My body grew into the form that my Maker designed it to be. But I've struggled with the belief that unless I am physically "perfect"—a perfection that is unattainable and unrealistic— I'm somehow not as valuable as everybody else. Barbie moved out, but Victoria moved in.

There's nothing quite like a glance at a Victoria's Secret catalog to invoke a flood of insecurities and feelings of disappointment. I know I'm supposed to be admiring the undergarments on those pages, and I can appreciate a well-made brassiere. But frankly, it isn't a well-made product that draws my attention. It's Victoria's models. Immediately a body comparison game ensues. Am I supposed to look like that? Those legs? That tummy? That skin? eyes? lips? My hair won't do that. And I know that bra wouldn't look that way on me.

It seems I'm not alone in my twisted worldview. A recent survey found that 70 percent of women felt depressed, guilty and shameful after looking at a fashion magazine for only three minutes. Even women who look as if they came from a lingerie ad are susceptible to questioning their worth in relationship to their appearance. Few of us are unaffected by the desire for a "body by Victoria."

How have I been affected by the desire
for a "body by Victoria"?

ஐ❧

ROLE MODELS AND COVER MODELS

It takes only a quick stroll past a magazine rack or a flip of the remote control to notice that our culture makes a clear statement. The ideal woman is beautiful. I mean drop-dead gorgeous. And if I want to reach "ideal" status, then my role models are those whom our culture has enthroned as the beautiful ones.

Here is where the lie begins. We confuse role models with cover models. We have taken on a cultural physics equation that says our value is directly proportional to our physical attractiveness. The result? We are people consumed with our outward appearance. And it shows.

There is nothing quite as revealing of our values as the ledger of our checkbooks. Each year, billions of dollars are spent in the quest to come just a bit closer to our culture's ideal beauty: $20 billion on cosmetics, $2 billion on hair products, $74 billion on diet foods. (Explain that to the hungry children of Sudan.) The beauty industry knows about our spending habits and therefore invests heavily in advertising campaigns. Magazine advertising revenue for cosmetics, beauty aids and hair products has reached over $1.5 billion a year. In addition, 7.4 million Americans spend a small fortune on cosmetic surgery annually. Five out of six of them are women.

We've been buying a lie. Literally. It's this: Being attractive means being happy. It means being admired, respected, loved. It means I have great value. Guys will want me. Girls will want to be me. Employers will hire me. Peers will befriend me.

Unfortunately, the lie is reinforced in everyday life: the culture's "beautiful ones" sometimes do get better treatment. Who hasn't noticed the way some guys gawk at a pretty girl? In high school the benefits of popularity—the prom queen or class president title, party invitations, dates—were lavished upon the pretty ones. TV shows like Donald Trump's *The Apprentice* gave us an inside glimpse at how women could use their good looks to close a business deal. I once saw an ad in *Ebony* magazine for hair relaxer that capitalized on the fact that a woman's appearance plays a significant role in landing a job: "Was it her résumé . . . or Raveen?" The relationship between people's looks and the way they are treated has even been a topic of psychological research. In one study, a "beautiful" woman and an "ugly" woman each approach an occupied phone booth where a dime was planted. When asked about the dime, 87 percent of booth occupants return it to the "beautiful" woman, but only 64 percent give it to the "ugly" one.

⌖ We have begun to confuse role models with cover models.

No wonder we're willing to pay whatever the cost for beauty. *Glamour* magazine did a survey asking, "What would you give up if you could slim down permanently?" Would you believe that 5 percent of respondents were actually willing to give up five years of their life?

From where we're standing, the grass certainly appears greener under the feet of a supermodel. But does physical beauty really deliver all that it promises us? Have we even stopped to notice?

The lie has us running full speed ahead, only to discover it's merely a mirage. For the images of beauty that we are chasing are not real women at all. Yes, that's right. The woman you saw last week on the cover of *Vogue*—the one with the voluptuous cleavage, the killer thighs, the flawless face, hair blowing in the wind over the caption in bold letters "JUST 5 DAYS TO THE PERFECT BODY"—she doesn't really exist.

I wonder if this is Victoria's big secret. The media industry uses a variety of deceptive techniques to create artificial beauty. We can't see the duct tape holding a model's chest in a gravity-defying position or the hemorrhoid cream used to fix her puffy, unrested eyes. Professionals are paid big bucks to spend hours on the model's makeup, hairstyling and wardrobe, using products and assistants that most of us will never have access to. My bathroom doesn't have professional lighting to highlight my best features and hide others. Even if it did, I can't hide out there forever. And let's be honest. If we saw a woman in line at the grocery store in a flattering pose like those we see on magazine covers, we'd think she was nuts.

> *I wonder if this is Victoria's big secret.*

As if those techniques weren't enough to "enhance" the model's beauty, the media industry then takes the photos and alters them electronically. They'll take a little off her tummy, airbrush out that cellulite and touch up her not-quite perfect complexion. The result is a completely fictitious image. Actress Julianne Moore agrees: "There is so much illusion in photographs and movies. I know an actress friend who was looking at a photo in a magazine and said, 'Why don't I look like that?'—and then she realized it was a picture of herself."

Most of us can't possibly come close to these images. Genetically our bodies just can't do it, and in many cases it wouldn't even be healthy. In the past three decades, most Miss America winners have had a body mass index that lies within the range of malnutrition. Actress Melanie Griffith has spent over fifty thousand dollars on plastic surgery on her tummy, thighs and hips. *Baywatch* legend Pamela Anderson admits to having had multiple liposuctions to reach emaciated proportions as well as enlarging her breasts. Many celebrities who are considered a bit heavy are actually underweight for their height and age. The average North American woman is 5 feet 3 inches tall and weighs 152 pounds. The average model is 5 feet 9 inches tall and weighs just 110 pounds. We've been comparing our bodies to fictitious, unhealthy or surgically altered ones.

How have I bought into the lies of the beauty culture?

℘♥

THE LIE EXPOSED

Believe it or not, the unthinkable has happened. Like a tiny hole torn out of the blindfold of humanity, a particle of reality made its way into the mass media. I was just an unsuspecting passerby when I stumbled upon the scandalous exposé.

The air was crisp on a sunny autumn day when I casually strolled into the brand-new Barnes & Noble that had just opened in town. As I was savoring the delicious aromas of new books and cappuccino, I started on my favorite route, beginning at the display tables just inside the door and making my way past the magazine racks. Let's see, *Rolling Stone?* Not today. *Cat Fancy?* Not ever. And then I saw it.

More magazine had done an interview and photo shoot with movie star Jamie Lee Curtis. Normally I would have breezed right past this article, but something was radically different about this spread. On one page Jamie Lee was posed in typical celebrity style that screamed, "Don't you want to be me?" Her skin was flawless. Her body was stunning in a sexy black dress and high heels. Three assistants surrounded her, touching up her trendy hairstyle and glamorous makeup. But right next to it was another photo of Jamie Lee. She had allowed photographers to shoot her in a sports bra and spandex briefs—no hairstyle, no makeup, no computer touchups, no special lighting and no apologies, tummy rolls and all.

Jamie Lee Curtis, the actress made famous by the movie *Perfect*, was revealing to the world that she isn't. The article quoted her saying, "There's a reality to the way I look without my clothes on. I don't have great thighs. I have very big breasts and a soft, fatty little tummy. And I've got back fat. People assume that I'm walking around in little spaghetti-strap dresses. It's insidious—Glam Jamie, the Perfect Jamie, the great figure, blah, blah, blah. . . . It's such a fraud. And I'm the one perpetuating it."

I scanned the faces of the cover models staring at me from that magazine rack. It was a sea of flawless perfection. Virtually every issue—*People, Glamour, Ebony, Latina, TV Guide*—was adorned with an image of the perfect hair, the perfect lips or the perfect cleavage. The photo of Jamie Lee Curtis was a refreshing glimpse of reality—well, close anyway. Even Jamie Lee has admitted to having plastic surgery. But amid all the smoke and mirrors, it was as though little Toto had pulled back the curtain of the Great Oz of Beauty, and the image was exposed as a fraud.

> 🖋 "It's insidious— Glam Jamie, the Perfect Jamie, the great figure, blah, blah, blah. . . . It's such a fraud. And I'm the one perpetuating it."
>
> <small>JAMIE LEE CURTIS, ACTRESS</small>

Almost immediately people were buzzing about Jamie Lee's daring photo shoot. Television giants like Oprah and Jay Leno interviewed her. Mail poured in to *More* magazine from readers who claimed their lives had been changed by the piece. After polling its readers, the magazine reported that 90 percent were elated that Jamie Lee had bared her true self. But when asked, "Would you have the courage to reveal yourself to public scrutiny?" 72 percent said, "Are you kidding? No chance."

And the very next issue of the magazine included "secrets of the stars" for achieving sleek hair and flawless skin. The curtain fell back into place, and we were back to smoke and mirrors.

FROM PARTNERS TO PINUPS

It hasn't always been this way. So how did we become so entangled in the lie? Although most historical eras have brought some particular definition of beauty standards, the mess we find ourselves in is actually a relatively recent phenomenon.

In her book *The Beauty Myth*, Naomi Wolf cites the Industrial Revolution as a key turning point in the way women's worth was measured.

> Before the development of technologies of mass production—daguerreotypes, photographs, etc.—an ordinary woman was exposed to few such images [of beauty] outside the Church. Since the family was a productive unit and women's work complemented men's, the value of women who were not aristocrats or prostitutes lay in their work skills, economic shrewdness, physical strength, and fertility. Physical attraction obviously played its part; but "beauty" as we understand it was not, for ordinary women, a serious issue in the marriage marketplace.

Industrialization took the husband's work away from home, and the emerging factories and businesses gave rise to the concepts of "breadwinner" and mere "domestic" work. As the middle class grew, the standard of living rose, families became smaller, and women found themselves comparatively idle. In addition, the invention of mass printing birthed a new era of visual images of perceived beauty. Wolf explains,

> Most of our assumptions about the way women have always thought about "beauty" date from no earlier than the 1830's,

when the cult of domesticity was first consolidated and the beauty index invented. For the first time new technologies could reproduce . . . images of how women should look. In the 1840's the first nude photographs of prostitutes were taken; advertisements using images of "beautiful" women first appeared in mid-century. Copies of classical artworks, postcards of society beauties and royal mistresses, Currier and Ives prints, and porcelain figurines flooded the separate sphere to which middle-class women were confined.

The ideal beauty queen was now in print. And she was in mass circulation. It's no wonder that women quickly began the comparison game. Once well-matched work partners with men, women were now measured not by their giftedness but by how closely they could emulate the women imaged in the media. And in a nation that prides itself on capitalism, it's no surprise that industry and advertising profited from the comparison game. Making money off women's new obsession would prove to be quite lucrative. And so the web was woven.

WHO'S THE BAD GUY?

Every story has a villain. It would be very easy to label the big bad media as the culprit. After all, aren't they the ones making a buck off our drive to be attractive? Aren't they the ones perpetuating the lie? Well, it isn't quite so simple.

A college friend of mine, Kristy,* and I bonded over everything from torturous psychology exams to late-night pizza orders. We shared secrets. We shared clothing. We also shared a common disdain for our figures. We would throw around lighthearted comments like, "Move over, sister. Make room on that couch for my Shamu-sized booty!"

I noticed, though, that Kristy's joking would escalate after she returned from breaks at home. Then I met her mother. Though Kristy's mom was quite friendly, no conversation with her lasted long before

---

*Her name, like the names of others mentioned in this book, has been changed.

the subject of body size inevitably came up. Who had lost weight. Who had gained weight. Calorie counting. Fat grams. What so-and-so should or should not have been wearing. And it wasn't long before her mom was comfortable with addressing me directly about it: "Have you lost weight, Michelle?" Of course I hadn't. Not with our steady diet of Lucky Charms, pepperoni pizza and the chocolate-chip cookies in my care package from home. I suppose it was her way of encouraging me to look my best. But instead it made me feel rotten about my body.

How Does It Start?

Though a sea of media-promoted artificial beauty surrounds us, it is actually those closest to us who do the most damage. We pass on our body obsessions to each other like a nasty strain of influenza. New research shows that feelings about body image start very early, long before the media play a significant role in girls' lives. A survey at Kenyon College discovered that elementary-school girls who were more concerned about body shape and weight were more likely to have mothers who made weight-related comments. The study quoted Ira Sacker (coauthor of *Dying to Be Thin*): "Some of my patients, who are just out of nursery school, tell me that they're fat. Turns out that their moms are saying the same thing about themselves."

One woman, Deborah, can't remember anyone telling her to be ashamed of her body. Not in so many words. It's easy to assume she's just been the victim of a Hollywood conspiracy. But look closer.

Deb comes from an interethnic family. Her Caucasian father had always struggled with his weight. They lived near Lake Michigan, and his embarrassment would always surface during summer months when the family would spend lots of time in swimsuits while boating and enjoying the beach. Her dad's feelings about his own body would occasionally spill over in comments about Deborah's. Deb remembers her father encouraging her to watch her weight when she was just twelve years old. Her muscular physique reflected her athletic lifestyle. But most other girls her age were stick-straight. She concluded that her bulging thighs must be fat. She spent adolescence feeling ugly and overweight.

Deborah's mother is Jewish. Deb remembers her mother's remarks about how unfortunate it was that she had passed on her "Jewish nose." The family considered plastic surgery for Jewish girls almost a rite of passage into womanhood. Deb's mom did it, her older sisters did it, aunts, cousins, friends, everyone. Her family even talked about giving Deb plastic surgery as a gift for her sixteenth birthday. Naturally Deborah assumed that her nose would be a hindrance to success and acceptance.

> ✐ We pass on our body obsessions to each other like a nasty strain of influenza.

Had the big bad media caused Deborah to dislike her body? Certainly we can't rule out our culture's influence on definitions of beauty and value, especially a culture so saturated with twisted perceptions about beauty and ethnicity—so saturated that as recently as 1996 a plastic surgery manual described procedures for altering ethnic noses, with specific directions for correcting a "Jewish nose."

But the influence of Deb's friends and family was even more contagious than the media. Unfortunately our loved ones are often oblivious to the wounds they inflict. In fact they sometimes think that their comments are an act of love. At age seventeen, Alice Chung wrote about her despair in struggling with an eating disorder:

> My mother tells me that I've been diagnosed with depression. My father tells me this is okay. That maybe God in all his holiness let this happen so that I could help others. . . . He tells me to pray. Pray, Alice. Pray. Ask him to help you and make you better. Pray. And then he points to my waist and tells me it's too thick. He says that I should lose some weight. I don't need him to tell me.

*In what ways have my family and friends affected
how I feel about my appearance?*

HOW ABOUT YOU?

How have you been affected by the lie that your body must fit a certain standard in order to be accepted? Check all of the following statements that apply to you:

☐ I am critical of my body.

☐ When I look in the mirror, I first notice the parts of my body that I think are inadequate.

☐ When I see images of "beautiful women" in the media, I compare myself to them.

☐ As I get dressed and ready in the morning, I consider what others will think of my appearance.

☐ I weigh myself frequently and am emotionally affected by the results.

☐ The thought of being seen without makeup or hair done is scary to me.

☐ When others compliment my appearance, I have a hard time believing it's true.

☐ When I eat in front of other people, I wonder what they are thinking about me.

☐ I tend to wear clothes that are baggy to hide my figure or tight clothes to show off my body in hopes of receiving attention.

☐ If money were no object, I would have plastic surgery in a heartbeat.

☐ I have often thought that becoming more beautiful would be the so-

lution to some of life's challenges—my desires for romantic relationships, career success, popularity among friends or self-esteem.

☐ In the past month I have spent a significant amount of money on
   beauty supplies.

If you checked eight to twelve of these statements, clearly it's time
for the Lord to begin to replace the cultural lies with his truth about
your body. Too many of us have fully bought the lie that our value is
directly proportional to our physical attractiveness. We need to pray
that the Lord would use this book to bring us freedom.

If you checked four to seven of these statements, you too have
been affected by the cultural lies about our bodies. You are not a full-
force beauty addict, but the danger still lurks that the lies could take
root in your soul and take over your life and relationships. Pray that
God would weed out those lies as you read and respond.

If you checked three or fewer of these statements, you're doing relatively well in a world that bombards us with false messages about
our bodies. Pray not only that God would use this book to encourage
you in your journey but also that you could be an agent of truth to
those around you who are struggling to love their bodies.

A NEW FAMILY INFLUENCE

It seems as though we're doomed. Bombarded by media. Infected by
those we love. Isn't it hopeless? Am I sentenced to a life of wishing I
were something that I'm not? A life of always falling short, always
feeling inadequate?

What if the insecure words of an overweight father were replaced
by loving words of truth from our heavenly Father? What if a family
encouraging us to obsess about our appearance were silenced by the
family of God's encouragements to love what God made and take care
of it well? What if friendships full of jokes about our bodies were
transformed by the Creator who calls us his friend? What if the definition of beauty authored by the Gap was edited by the definition of

beauty created by the Author of Life? David knew the answer. He was able to shout at the top of his lungs, "You knit me together in my mother's womb. I praise you because *I am fearfully and wonderfully made;* your works are wonderful, I know that full well" (Psalm 139:14). Sure, he never had to shop for jeans or compete with Halle Berry. But what if we were able to shout with him, with complete sincerity, each morning while getting dressed and ready for the day? Some might say these are childish dreams of a reality that will never exist—a dream world not far beyond candy necklaces and Barbie. But what if?

What if the insecure words of an overweight father were replaced by loving words of truth from our heavenly Father?

What would it take to fully agree with David that "I am fearfully and wonderfully made"?

TOOLS FOR THE JOURNEY

As I have journeyed with Jesus, he has been faithful to walk me through a process of changing how I feel about my body. Though his work in me is not over, there are three incredible tools God has used to reconstruct my body image, and I've included all three in this book.

The first has been ongoing conversation with God. I used to think that "meeting with God" meant reading a bit of my Bible and sending up a grocery-list prayer for needs that he should know about already. But my time with God has been transformed into an intimate time of conversation. I learned how to let God speak to me through Scripture. I learned how to hear his voice in prayer. I learned to converse with him by journaling.

My journals were not for recording the day's events to look back on later. They were to help me process my life and slow me down to hear God. I would allow God to ask me questions about my life that I would answer in my journal. As I journaled, I would pause periodically to process what I had just written, giving God time to respond to my soul.

In each chapter of this book you'll find reflection questions sprinkled throughout. I encourage you to use them to begin a journal in which you set out to converse with God about healthy body image. Write down your thoughts, and give God time to talk to you about those things.

The second tool I discovered was Scripture memory. I used to think that memorizing Bible verses was a tedious exercise reserved for kids in Sunday school. But that changed in my sophomore year of college. At the time I was really struggling with a lustful thought life. One day my InterVarsity staff worker said something that I will never forget: "When you are struggling with sin, the best weapon is to memorize a truth in the Bible that speaks to that particular issue. Then when you are tempted, recite the Bible verse. Soon you will find victory, because the last thing that Satan wants to do is to tempt you with something that will trigger Scripture!" I noticed, too, that this was Jesus' response to temptation. When Satan tempted him in the desert, how did he respond? With Scripture.

So I set out to memorize Philippians 4:8, "Finally, brothers, whatever is true, whatever is noble, whatever is right, whatever is pure, whatever is lovely, whatever is admirable—if anything is excellent or praiseworthy—think about such things." Then every time I found my mind wandering to lustful thoughts, I would recite this verse, sometimes even out loud. And you know, it wasn't long before I found freedom. I really was thinking about "such things."

Likewise, certain verses have been quite influential in transforming my body image. That's why at the end of each chapter I suggest a Scripture to memorize. I pray that as you memorize these words God would brand the truth on your heart.

The third tool is community. God never intended for us to live alone, nor should we think that we can become more like Jesus on our own. God's Word tells us, "Now you are the body of Christ, and each one of you is a part of it" (1 Corinthians 12:27). "The eye cannot say to the hand, 'I don't need you!' And the head cannot say to the feet, 'I don't need you!'" (12:21). The quest for a healthy body image requires us to swim against the current of mainstream culture. It has been invaluable to have others diving in alongside me.

At the end of each chapter I include some questions for discussion. While the personal reflection questions are designed for you to use alone with God, the discussion questions are meant to help you process the material with other people. It is my hope that you will find others to read and discuss the material with you and that you'll find strength and encouragement as you discover that you are not striving alone. Maybe you will be surprised to find someone shares your struggles. Maybe you will experience healing as you let yourself be vulnerable and open up to others some things you've kept private. Maybe it will be an opportunity to build crosscultural friendships that both bless you and change our world. Maybe you will tap into the unique power of interceding in prayer for each other. Or maybe someone in a different place will offer you wisdom, hope or practical suggestions. Don't be one who says, "I don't need you!"

Our world already bulges with books, magazine articles and television interviews about establishing a healthy body image. But in these pages you will not find nutritional hype about carbohydrates, fashion tips for dressing your body type or ten easy steps to a prettier you. I believe that the core of the issue is spiritual. And God has plenty to say to us about it. The place to begin is to wrestle with some key biblical truths about how God made us and how much he delights in us. I have found very little hope for a truly healthy body image outside of knowing Jesus intimately. Sure, there are therapists and an endless supply of self-help books. But these can be mere Band-Aids on the real problems deep within us. The problems are actually the result of human rebellion, our turning away from a loving God and his loving plans for us. The Bible calls this sin, and we all have rebellious hearts. It is only through Jesus that our rebellion finds remedy.

You likely won't agree with everything I say. That's OK. But I believe that God wants to speak to us. I believe that God grieves for the joy and freedom we are missing when we attempt to live by values dictated by the culture. I believe we have bought a lie, but the Lord of grace, the One whose job it is to make old things new and dead things alive, desires to change the parts of us we think are hopelessly unchangeable. That is why I love him so much. May you encounter God's great love for you on these pages and fall deeper in love with him too.

SCRIPTURE TO MEMORIZE

For you created my inmost being; you knit me together in my mother's womb. I praise you because I am fearfully and wonderfully made; your works are wonderful, I know that full well.
PSALM 139:13-14

QUESTIONS FOR DISCUSSION

1. How do you think the culture has defined beauty?

2. What images of beauty have most affected you?

3. In what ways have you bought into the lie that being attractive will make you happy, likable or successful? How does that affect your life on a daily basis?

4. What would it take for you to have the same vulnerable confidence that Jamie Lee Curtis displayed?

5. In what ways have you seen messages about body image passed down through your family?

6. What would be different in your life if you experienced the freedom of living out Psalm 139?

2 ❧ WAS EVE A 36C?

Beauty and the Fall

BEAUTY IS THE MARK OF THE WELL MADE,

WHETHER IT BE A UNIVERSE OR AN OBJECT.

❧ *Thomas Aquinas*

A table for nine was going to take about thirty minutes, but we didn't mind. The late summer sun was still shining. The extra time just meant plenty of laughter, good conversation and the wonderful smell of deep-dish pizza wafting through the air.

As we were in a public place with a rather large group, my "mom radar" kicked in after a bit, and I decided to take a quick inventory of our family. My husband was standing by the door, chuckling and exchanging computer stories. Our eight-week-old son was resting soundly in his arms. Our daughter was on a bench across the sidewalk, entertaining a few of our friends with gripping tales of Copper the dog, her imaginary friend. *All is well.* Relieved, I resumed conversation with the friend sitting next to me.

But it was only a matter of seconds before I heard a panicked cry for help. "Mommy, Mommy! Look! I don't like it!" Natalie, our daughter, ran to me with tears streaming down her cheeks. What could possibly have caused such a crisis in her three-year-old world?

"What's wrong, sweetheart?" I asked as I embraced her on my lap.

"Look. There's a spot on my finger. I don't like it. Get it off! Get it off!" she whimpered between sniffles.

Expecting to find a bug bite or the beginnings of leprosy, I inspected the affliction. She was pointing to a freckle that had made its home on the inside of her tiny ring finger.

"Oh, honey, it's OK. It's just a freckle. It won't hurt you," I promised.

"No, Mommy, I don't like it. Get it off," she protested.

"Natalie, it's OK. This spot makes you special. See, Mommy has spots too. They make me special. God gave you that spot because it's beautiful, and it makes you special, sweetie."

But Natalie wouldn't hear it. She had made up her mind that she didn't like it. For days we had the same conversation over and over about the terrible spot.

"I don't like it. Get it off."

"It's beautiful. It makes you special."

"But Mommy, I don't like it."

I couldn't understand what would make my daughter obsess over such a tiny detail on her body. Objectively there was nothing wrong with it. It wouldn't hurt her. Most people would never even notice it. There's nothing remotely freakish about it. It's just a freckle. No big deal.

But don't we do the same thing? How many times in my life have I become overly sensitive about parts of my body that objectively are just fine? I still remember the day in junior high when *I* discovered a large freckle had appeared on the left side of my nose. I hated that freckle. It was so large and distracting that it might as well have had a blinking red light to warn low-flying aircraft not to run into it.

To this day, however, no one has ever commented on my obtrusive freckle. I doubt most people have even noticed it. Over the years I have become much less concerned about my freckle, but other parts of my body have brought me just as much discontent.

Have I become overly sensitive about particular body parts?

Now as Natalie was expressing a hauntingly similar body anxiety, I began to wonder if she had learned it from me. As intentional as my husband and I had been about telling her she was loved, that she was smart and talented, that she was beautiful and special, had my own insecurities already begun rubbing off on her? I remembered how she had tried to mimic me putting on makeup by the time she was two years old. I thought about our daily routine of doing her hair before we went out anywhere. I tried to remember flippant comments I had made about my body while pregnant with her younger brother. Had I already tainted Natalie in her three short years of life?

Maybe I had. But maybe there was also something innate in her that would cause her to reject her God-created body. It doesn't make sense. How could such a beautiful and special little girl think she's not beautiful and special? She isn't the first female to have done that. In fact, even the very first woman, Eve, expressed similar behavior. Let's take a look.

In the Beginning

I've often heard supermodels reveal in interviews that they aren't very satisfied with their appearance. Supermodel icon Christie Brinkley remembers, "When I did my first *Sports Illustrated*, I was squirming, thinking, 'How can I hide my heavy thighs? How can I conceal these wide hips?'" Absurd, isn't it? Obvious beauties who don't like the way they look.

The story that God tells us about Eve is just as curious, involving another beauty queen who is ashamed of the way she looks. The narrative of Genesis 1—3 is an ironic melodrama and ultimately reveals that we aren't the first generation of women to have issues with our bodies.

As the curtain opens, we see our Master Creator at work. Light and dark are being made from nothing. At the mere spoken word of the

Lord, *boom!* We have sky, and seas, and land. *Pow!* Stars, the sun, the moon. The mountains and oceans take their places at his command.

ℒ✔ We aren't the first generation of women to have issues with our bodies.

With delight he forms the majestic Andes, the massive redwoods and the sand-waves of the Mojave. The Artist uses his richly hued palate to add color and depth and beauty that steal your breath.

Then he gets really creative—birds and fish, plants and animals. Not just one kind of each, either. Doves and chickens, penguins and ostrich. Poodles and Labradors, Chihuahuas and St. Bernards. "Hmmm, I think I'll make camels spit. I think I'll make male seahorses the ones to get pregnant instead of the females." The Maker defines creativity like no one else. And after each brushstroke he declares, "Now that's good."

But do you remember what happens next? He creates us. Male and female he creates us. In his image he creates us. He forms every curve, every skin cell, every lash and ligament. Afterward he says, "Now this . . . this is *very* good." God looks at all he has made. It's breathtaking. Phenomenal. Then he turns to humanity. And in light of all else he has made, he declares us his masterpiece. We are the only thing God made that wasn't just good but *very good* (Genesis 1:31).

Savor that for a minute. There was something about being fashioned to reflect the image of God himself that made us the pinnacle of creation. Our soul, our temperament, our emotions, our gender, and yes, even our body were all designed to reflect the One who made us. Judith Couchman writes that we were "formed in the likeness of the flawless, holy, loving, compassionate, omniscient, powerful God. Though Scripture doesn't give details about [Adam and Eve's] appearance and personalities, for man and woman to be created in God's image implies they modeled his perfection. Their bodies, minds, and souls exhibited his highest ideal for humanity, for all of creation."

There is something about us that collectively bears the mark of our Creator. Tall, short, curvy, straight, slim, thick, dark, light, sleek, kinky, freckled or porcelain: we are the image of a creative and beautiful God. Asian, European, African, Latino, multiracial and Native peoples all bear the unique fingerprint of our Creator. Adhering to one physical standard of beauty is like throwing a bucket of bleach onto a Michelangelo masterpiece. Calling that a tragedy would be an understatement.

> *✐* There is something about us that collectively bears the mark of our Creator.

The first time I visited Chicago's Art Institute, I saw a painting that has stuck in my mind ever since. I am no art critic, but even I could appreciate its genius. It was Georges Seurat's *La Grande Jatte,* an enormous painting of a park filled with people on a warm summer day. It looks lush and inviting. The scene is serene and colorful; people are enjoying the sunlit waterside and tender family moments. But when I stepped closer, I noticed the brilliance of Seurat's technique. Nose to canvas, I realized that he hadn't used confident sweeping brushstrokes but tiny little dots. Each dot has a life of its own. Each is placed perfectly, intentionally and with precision. The artist chose with care the location, the size and the shade of each individual dot. Millions of dots later, they collectively form a breathtaking picture that communicates beauty, emotion and intensity. Together they make an image that is unforgettable. So do we.

Had just one of those dots decided to change its color or size, had it decided it needed to look just like the dot seventeen spaces to the left, the entire picture would have become distorted. In fact, anyone looking at the painting would be distracted by that one spot and might miss the wonder of the picture as a whole. Isn't this what we

do to the image of God stamped on us? I decide that the way I look
is a tragic mistake—if only I could look like her over there or change
these "problem spots," this art piece would be much improved. Our
bodies were designed not only with care but with the purpose of reflecting the image of God to a world that claims he is nowhere to be
found.

*What would help me remember that my body is part of a bigger
picture of humanity that collectively bears God's image?*

POETRY AND ROSES

Humanity was created precisely and lovingly to reflect the image of
the Creator. In chapter 2 of Genesis the camera zooms in to give us a
telephoto view of God's artistry in making us. If God himself rejoiced
at our completion, it's no wonder that next we see Adam responding
to Eve with amazed pleasure.

The Lord had already made it clear that his image was fully expressed in making both men and women (Genesis 1:27). Now we see
that he also envisioned a unique partnership. The first dilemma in
Scripture arises: Adam is alone and it isn't good (Genesis 2:18). God's
image is incomplete, for humans need community. So the Lord begins the task of making the first female body.

While Adam is under divine anesthesia, God takes a piece of
Adam's side to begin the process. Eve is made from the same stuff
Adam is. She isn't taken from his head or his feet, places of symbolic
honor or servitude. Instead the Lord forms her from Adam's side. She
will be his partner, his companion. God starts with a piece of Adam's
body, and he completes her form with the same care and creativity
with which he built Adam from a starter mix of dirt. Then God pre-
sents her to the man like a proud father walking his daughter down
the aisle.

I wonder what Eve looked like. What shade was God's first female dot on the canvas of humanity? Was she tall and thin? Was she full and voluptuous? Did she have long, thick eyelashes? Was she the optimal 36C? Did her hair flow Pantene-like in the warm Eden breeze?

The truth is that it doesn't seem to matter. For Adam's response tells it all. The man wakes from his slumber. God unveils his masterpiece. Adam flips out.

"Bone of my bones and flesh of my flesh; she shall be called 'woman,' for she was taken out of man" (Genesis 2:23). Adam is so filled with awe at his first glance that he bursts into spontaneous poetry. And it doesn't appear that he is rejoicing over Eve's personality. They hadn't spent days or weeks getting to know one another at this point. Adam has yet to discover the beauty God has made in a woman's soul. While God is filling humanity's need for partnership and Adam is grateful for a companion who isn't a platypus, he is rejoicing after one look at her beautiful body.

> *I wonder what Eve looked like. What shade was God's first female dot on the canvas of humanity?*

I wonder what it was like to be Eve in that moment. God forms her and then tells her it's time to meet her partner. Scripture doesn't mention it, but I doubt that Eve got time to primp before her blind date. Anyway, why would she need to improve on what God had just finished putting together?

Then came the moment of truth. *What will Adam think of me?*

Some of us live our whole life with that question dangling over our head. *If I go to school in these jeans, what will they think of me? When I see that cute guy again today, what will he think of me? When I run to the store without makeup, what will they think of me? When I visit my aunt this weekend, will she mention how I look? What will she think of me?*

*When am I most concerned with what
others will think of my appearance?*

ℒ♥

I remember that feeling on my wedding night. I stressed about it
for months beforehand. There I would be, completely unveiled before my partner. Every inch of me exposed. *What will he think of me?
Will he shrink back in disappointment? Will he be polite and avoid looking
at the parts I'd rather hide? Will he tolerate my imperfections?* I was sure
we would vow our lives at the ceremony, celebrate at the reception,
and then go to our hotel room to "unwrap" the gift God had given to
each of us, only for my new husband to feel like somehow he'd gotten the shaft. "Oh," he'd say, pausing awkwardly, "did you save the
receipt?"

But when God takes a look at us, he isn't disappointed. When we
bare ourselves before God, he responds not by merely tolerating and
accepting us but by rejoicing over our magnificent beauty. Thankfully,
so did my husband. And so did Adam. What relief and freedom Eve
must have felt in the moment Adam became a rose-bearing poet.

ℒ♥ **If only we understood the magnificent gift of our God-made body. Maybe we could quit holding our breath in fear of being rejected.**

If only we understood the magnificent gift of our God-made body.
Maybe we could quit holding our breath in fear of being rejected.
Maybe we could know more joy and freedom in our relationships. And
maybe we would treat our body differently.

I remember fondly one family vacation when I was sixteen years
old. My dad and I sneaked away and were spending a special after-
noon together window-shopping. I spotted a jewelry store and began

to admire a simple emerald ring with two tiny diamonds hugging the stone in the middle.

"Would you like it?" Dad said with a grin.

"Are you serious? It's expensive, Dad!" I gasped in disbelief.

It wasn't a special occasion. We hadn't been planning to buy anything that day. I certainly didn't think we could afford it. But my dad quietly strolled into the store and came out with a tiny ring box in his hand—just because.

I love that ring. Not just because it's pretty but because it represents my father's deep love for me. It was a beautiful gift. So naturally I wasn't ashamed to wear it. I agreed joyfully when others complimented it. I never worried over whether so-and-so thought it looked nice. I took good care of it, cleaning and protecting it. And though I delighted in it, I didn't compare it to other people's jewelry or try to flaunt it. My life didn't revolve around the ring. I just quietly savored the loving gift that it was.

When we understand the gift of our God-made body, we will respond the same way: with contentment and without embarrassment. We will take care of our body well by eating healthy foods and giving it the exercise of an active lifestyle. We'll keep ourselves clean and enjoy pampering our body, without crossing the line into body obsessions or comparing ourselves to other women. And we'll be free from wondering, *What will they think of me?* For our body is a gift from a loving Father.

*How might I take better care of my body
if I saw it as a gift of love?*

᠊᠊

FROM SHALOM TO SHAME

Genesis 2 ends by summarizing it all: "The man and his wife were both naked, and they felt no shame" (Genesis 2:25). Their bodies were completely exposed, yet they were completely unashamed. They rested in the wisdom and skill of their Designer. Couchman writes, "If we understand that everything is created by a perfect God and declared good and holy, we're not bent on changing ourselves. We are free to be."

Refreshing, isn't it, the thought of living in a world of complete contentment with our bodies? Men and women frolic freely in the Garden of Eden, uninhibited by self-consciousness. They not only are comfortable with how they look but even write songs celebrating it. It's a life brimming with *shalom,* a Hebrew term that carries connotations of completeness, peace, well-being, security, justice and prosperity. Shalom is God's perfect, harmonious intention for creation.

The first man and woman are free to be. It sounds nothing like our plastic-surgery world. So what happened?

Unfortunately, the freedom didn't last long. Genesis goes on to tell about the tragic destruction of sin. Adam and Eve chose rebellion over God, and the consequences were immediate. With the crunch of forbidden fruit still in the air and juice dripping from their chins, "the eyes of both of them were opened, and they realized they were naked; so they sewed fig leaves together and made coverings for themselves" (Genesis 3:7).

It was doubt that had led them to rebel in the first place. The serpent whispered, "Did God really say, 'You must not eat from any tree in the garden'?" (Genesis 3:1). The truthful and faithful response would have been, "No. He only asked us not to eat from the tree that would cause death. His boundaries are for our good." But instead Eve began to doubt God's good intentions for them. She explained to the evil one that they couldn't eat from one particular tree, but added that they

✐ Is my body really as good as he says? The seeds of doubt begin to germinate.

couldn't touch it either. Not true. God never said that. Already she was painting him harsher than he is.

When the serpent tried to convince her that God had ulterior motives ("You will not surely die. . . . For God knows that . . . your eyes will be opened, and you will be like God," Genesis 3:4-5), Eve took the bait. She doubted God's good intentions for them. Crunch. And Adam fell for the lie about God just as quickly. Crunch. Drip.

Is God looking out for our best? Is he really as good as he says? Is my body really as good as he says? The seeds of doubt begin to germinate. If God isn't fully trustworthy, then why would I trust his intentions in making me?

The freedom of Eve and Adam's shalom began with an intimate trust that their Creator was good, holy and perfect. But when that trust was broken, the pieces fell like dominoes.

How have I doubted God's good intentions in making me?

L♥

The serpent is called "the father of lies." He lies about who God is. He lies about who we are. And when Adam and Eve fell for his deception, the result was an immediate sense of shame. They "realized" their nakedness, and the first fashion statement was made. Apparently fig leaves were the hot fabric trend of the season.

I find it interesting that first the couple hide their bodies, and only later do they hide themselves in the bushes. I would think that if their sin caused them solely to feel guilty over *what they had done,* they would have simply hidden from God in the bushes. They would have tried to hide only from the One they disobeyed. But instead they first attempt to hide *who they are.* They try to hide their very identities.

Psychologist Lewis Smedes notes, "The difference between guilt and shame is very clear—in theory. We feel guilty for what we *do.* We feel shame for what we *are.* A person feels guilt because he *did* something wrong. A person feels shame because he *is* something wrong."

According to Merle Fossum, "A pervasive sense of shame is the on-going premise that one is fundamentally bad, inadequate, defective, unworthy, or not fully valid as a human being."

I believe that at the root of our physical insecurities, shame is flourishing. This shame was sown by seeds of doubt. We wonder whether our Creator's work in creating our body was flawed: *By the time my DNA mix came together, God obviously had stopped creating bodies with precision and perfect loving artistry. God was not perfect in creating me. Nor am I a creation of God deemed "very good."*

To be clear, shame was not the only result of sin. The effects were so far-reaching that human beings were affected physically as well. Death and decay entered the world, and humanity has made sinful choices that render consequences for our bodies. But God remains sovereign as our Creator. Our fallen bodies still reflect his image, and God has still woven beauty into the fabric of our physicality. Instead of recognizing the effects of a fallen world, we sometimes conclude God to be an inadequate Creator. We doubt his goodness, and shame takes over.

The serpent slithers away satisfied, and we are left feeling defective and searching for fig leaves. Our shame tells us that we must hide our true selves. *If someone saw what I'm really like, surely they would judge me and reject me.* Our shame makes us hungry for praise, and we think we'll never get that affirmation with our body the way it is. Our reaction to this defective body is to hide it. We have made fig fashions of our own.

We hide behind our clothes, our hair, our makeup: the right label, the right cut, the right color, the right accessories, the right surgeon. We live by the rules: black is slimming; horizontal stripes are unflattering. Some of us buy clothes too large, hoping to hide our figure. Some of us buy clothes too tight, hoping to draw attention to particular body parts and win the affirmation we are starving for. Some of us must have the latest and trendiest clothes, hoping to make a statement that we are on top of the fashion food chain. Some of us want a more permanent hiding place and think plastic surgery is our only hope. Some of us would rather die than be caught without makeup done and hair styled. As one of my friends used to say, "Leave the house without lipstick? Are you kidding? I'd feel naked!"

We have made fig fashions of our own.

Oprah Winfrey once did an experiment and asked several women to go weeks without makeup. They cleared out their bathroom drawers and fasted from their Maybelline and Mary Kay. They later confessed to being filled with fear. They feared what people would think of them. They feared judgment. They feared exposing their imperfections. Overcome with self-consciousness, they desired to hide again behind makeup. But they resisted and pressed on with life au naturel.

The first few days were rough. They hadn't realized how dependent they had become on cosmetics to feel confident and acceptable. They braced themselves for the worst.

But the harsh rejection they had feared never came. Before long they found that they didn't really need the mask of makeup. They were no longer worried about other people's reactions. When the experiment was done, the women went back to their cosmetics but no longer felt an addictive dependency upon them. The choice to wear makeup now came from a desire to pamper their body instead of a desire to hide it.

THE ANTIDOTE FOR SHAME

Adam and Eve's story had tragic consequences. Hiding in shame. Banished from the garden. No longer frolicking in God's shalom. Humans had managed to destroy the perfect harmony of what God created. But the good news is that God spends the rest of Scripture revealing how he is using the power of grace to restore shalom and rescue us.

Shame has one enemy. It's called grace. Grace is unmerited favor from God. It is an unearned gift. It is the quintessential ingredient in God's kingdom. For those of us learning to follow Jesus, learning to live as a resident of God's community, it is the currency of life.

If shame tells me I am defective, grace tells me I am valuable. Shame's greatest weapon is the fear of judgment. Grace's even greater weapon is the relief of unconditional love. Shame says that because I am flawed I am unacceptable. Grace says that though I am flawed I am cherished. Shame believes that the opinion of others is what matters. Grace believes that the opinion of God is what matters. Shame claims I must be perfect to earn the approval of others. Grace claims I am accepted regardless of seeming imperfections. Shame makes us hide. Grace makes us frolic. Shame is the language of the serpent. Grace is the language of Jesus.

> ✍ Shame says that because I am flawed, I am unacceptable. Grace says that though I am flawed, I am cherished.

My relationship with God took a major turn postcollege when I realized how poorly I understood the currency of grace. I could recite Ephesians 2:8 with the best of them: "For it is by grace you have been saved, through faith—and this not from yourselves, it is the gift of God . . ." But I was living as though I needed to make God pleased with me. What I truly expected from God was disappointment; but if I did all the right Christian things, maybe I could make him happier with me. I applied this logic to other people as well. What I expected was judgment and rejection; but if I tried hard to be perfect, maybe I could make them pleased with me. I was swimming in the murky waters of shame, until God began to show me that this is not the way things work in his kingdom.

Luke 15 tells the story of a son who leaves his home to live it up on his own. But after a disappointing turn of events, he finds himself wallowing around with pigs, so hungry he wishes he could eat the slop out of their troughs.

He returns home. I can't imagine what he smelled like. And I'm sure his filthy appearance spoke his story of defeat. But his father does the unlikely. He runs to his son. Hugs the swine-reeking boy. Puts his own robe on the son's slimy body. And he throws a huge party to show him off.

I wonder if the boy showered before his big fiesta. If it were me, I would need a few days to get ready. *All those people at the party—I want them to accept me. I'll definitely need a hot bath, a shopping trip, a new haircut and a manicure. Those pods of pig feed were rough on the nails.*

The story doesn't say if the son cleans up. But what Jesus does want us to know is that it isn't his perfectly clean persona that earns the father's lavish affection. *Nothing* earns that love.

God had no intention for us to waste so much effort on trying to earn approval. So if we truly believe that he offers us a life marked by grace, will we live as though there is grace for us? Or will we continue to invest in our appearance, with the assumption that we'll encounter only harsh judgment?

Those who live in God's grace, Paul says, will be changed. "The grace of God that brings salvation has appeared to all men. It teaches us to say 'No' to ungodliness and worldly passions, and to live self-controlled, upright and godly lives in this present age" (Titus 2:11-12). When we realize that our bodies are made to collectively bear the image of God, we live free of the "worldly passion" of appearance obsession. When we rest in God's deep satisfaction in creating our body, we will stop worrying about what others think of us. When we know that our body is a priceless gift from a loving Father, we will take care of it well. When we live in the reality that God does not reject our body, we will stop hiding in shame.

Saturating my life with God's grace is the only antidote for the shame that began in the Garden of Eden. I really can taste a measure of the perfect peace God meant for me with the body I've been given. I don't have to fret about looking just right in order to be accepted. I already am. I don't have to hide behind the right jeans. I was made very good by a God who loves me and doesn't make mistakes. My hair is not a mistake. My nose is not a mistake. And neither is that freckle on the inside of a tiny ring finger.

A JOURNALING EXERCISE

One practical step we can take toward purging shame from our life is to identify the voices of shame that we have been listening to. Bringing those sources into the light will often strip them of power over us.

Take out a journal and spend some time thinking through the people and experiences that have been sources of shameful messages.

- What messages do you remember hearing about your body when you were a young girl? They might have come on the playground, at the dinner table, while buying school clothes, through toys you played with, when you were compared to siblings, etc.

- What messages were most memorable during your early teens? Think of messages you got in gym class, with your first bra, comments from family members, your dating life, beauty rituals passed on from Mom or Grandma, and so on.

- What recent experiences have communicated shameful messages about your body?

- How did these messages affect the way you view your body? What are your feelings toward the sources of these messages?

Journal your thoughts about the choices you have: what messages you listen to, what power you give to the sources of these messages, whether you live in shame or live in grace.

After identifying the sources of shame, spend some time praying that the Holy Spirit would begin a work of freeing you from the wounds they caused. Then ask God to replace your shameful feelings with an overwhelming sense of his grace for you.

SCRIPTURE TO MEMORIZE

So God created man in his own image,
in the image of God he created him;
male and female he created them.
GENESIS 1:27

QUESTIONS FOR DISCUSSION

1. Think back on your life. What is your earliest memory of discontentment with your body?

2. What does it mean to you that you are made to reflect the image of God?

3. If God meant us to be like painted dots on a great canvas, collectively bearing his full image, what can we learn about beauty from men and women of ethnicities different than ours?

4. What do you think it was like to be Eve in the garden before sin entered the picture?

5. How has shame influenced the way you live? your relationships? the way you view your body?

6. How would your body image be different if you lived by the standards of God's grace instead of shame?

7. What stood out to you in the comparisons of shame and grace?

8. What can you begin doing today to understand and live out that grace?

3 ✑ WHEN BEAUTY BECOMES A BEAST

Beauty and Consequences

*M*y freshman year at the University of Illinois I arrived on campus ready for the full college experience. Dorm life. New friends. Cute guys. Total freedom. Unfortunately there seemed to be two unavoidable hardships in the first year: the Freshman Fifteen and the required science credits. These credits were partly fulfilled by a biology course, which included dutiful study of human anatomy.

The strangest thing happened that year. On one hand, I worried about gaining the expected fifteen pounds and felt embarrassed about my appearance, and on the other, I learned more about the human body and grew to appreciate God as a Designer. It is beyond me how anyone could study the body and deny that a Master Artist created us.

My body can take a Chicken McNugget, dissolve it, sort it into its various components (I've heard it's best not to know what those are), send each ingredient to the appropriate destination, and turn it into energy fueling my muscles to carry me wherever I choose to go. And it does this without any conscious thought on my part. My immune system has the ability to keep track of nearly every microorganism that I've come into contact with and use that registry to create weaponry for future use. If for some reason I accidentally puncture my body, as I'm liable to do whenever my klutzy self passes the coffee table, it can actually fix itself. The body is a fascinating masterpiece.

And not just in a biochemical way. Our form is fascinating as well. Artists will never grow tired of trying to capture the beauty of the human body. Most art students at some point take a course requiring them to draw, paint or sculpt human figures.

Our bodies are intricate, complex and beautiful. They are gifts from the Lord that remind us of our awesome Creator.

All of these things I believe to be true of the body. So why do I have a hard time translating it to my own physique? Why did I spend that year appreciating the human body God designed while simultaneously disdaining my own? Many of us are suffering from a tragic disconnect that causes us to take God's gift for granted. We don't see ourselves as a work of art but as a collection of imperfections. God made humanity in general beautiful, but my body is an exception to the rule. It's as if God and I were having a conversation like this . . .

> ✒ Why did I spend that year appreciating the human body God designed while simultaneously disdaining my own?

GOD: Do you know that I made everything you see?

MICHELLE: Oh yes, Lord, and what a great job you did! Down to every last detail—bravo! Standing ovation, even.

GOD: Do you know that I made you too?

MICHELLE: Right. Good job. The human body is pretty amazing. And so is mine, well, all except for my hair. It's a little limp, and the color needs some livening up. But other than that—and my thighs don't look exactly swimsuit-ready. And now that I think about it, you could have improved slightly on my chest. It's not just like everybody else's. Oh, and my skin's too freckly, and there's the matter of my height, and my hips, and my eyes. Actually, God, I have a short performance review I've typed up for you that might help in your future people making. I mean, really, great job in general with humanity. But my particular body could have used a better design.

Unfortunately this attitude has substantial consequences. We can become tangled in the web of discontent, fear and perfectionism, leading us into unhealthy obsessions.

Do I believe that my body is a masterpiece created by a perfect God? Why or why not?

CRAVING OR CONTENTMENT

Have you ever known someone who exudes contentment? They're rare. I can think of only a few. Sonia is one of them. It's like she has a buffer zone of peace around her. It's not that nothing hard or painful ever happens to her, but she has this clarity of focus, this flexibility, this ability to laugh amidst difficulty, this deep satisfaction that doesn't change with the ups and downs of life. She rarely mentions her appearance, but she doesn't renounce makeup or wear a burlap sack.

Something happens when I'm with people like Sonia. They are so content with life, with who they are and what God is doing, that I can actually taste it. My soul exhales.

I bet the apostle Paul was like that. He wrote to his friends in Philippi that he has "learned the secret of being content in any and every situation" (Philippians 4:12). And he later counsels his buddy Timothy saying, "Godliness with contentment is great gain" (1 Timothy 6:6). I suspect that if we interviewed Paul about our dilemma, his letter back to us would begin with teaching on contentment (after a lengthy greeting, of course).

Contentment has been defined as a resting of the mind without craving something else. Looking at Paul, we see that contentment has much to do with Who or what we are gazing at. He was so in love with his Lord, so connected with God and so confident of his calling that minor details like whether he had any food or was being held prisoner didn't hold his attention. I doubt that he liked being in jail. But he was able to rejoice because of his intimacy with God. The concerns of life didn't disappear, but they weren't allowed to be in the spotlight.

A wise Jesuit understanding of life also points us toward contentment. In this view, all things in life—my work, my money, my body, my relationships—are tools for God's kingdom. They are important parts of life, but my heart is not tied to them. Being content is saying to God, "This is what you have for me, and I will be OK with that because I know you will ultimately use it to teach me and work toward your purposes in the world."

> ✒ The body God chose for each of us— our eyes, our hair, our chest, our calves— is actually not ours. It is a tool for the kingdom.

Such contentment lies just out of reach for those of us who are struggling to love our bodies. We spend so much thought, money and time craving another body. We have taken our eyes off God's good plans for us and for his kingdom. We have forgotten that the body God chose for each of us—our eyes, our hair, our chest, our calves—is actually not ours. It is a tool for the kingdom.

What would it be like for our heart to not be tied to our body parts—to stop obsessing over every detail we don't like? I think we'd find new freedom. I think we'd experience the bigness of God's plans in the world. I think we'd take better care of our body. I think we'd find that godliness with contentment really is great gain.

Being discontent with what we look like can sometimes make us discontent with our position in life too. There was an unspoken equation that I learned as a single woman: my chance of getting married correlates directly with my physical attractiveness. With this line of reasoning, if we're not content about how we look, we won't be content with our singleness either. We think that being single is a result of rejection. But singleness is not a default status for the rejected. It is a place where a loving God has us for a reason. We may have a hard time deciphering this, though, if we've felt rejected.

When my friend Sarah started dating Todd, she was typically giddy. Todd was a fun guy, the kind that girls would meet once and immediately wonder if they stood a chance at a date. The two dated for quite a while, and Sarah began to daydream about what features she would choose on her white gown. Then Todd announced that he wouldn't marry her because he thought her legs were too fat.

Sarah was devastated. Her legs were actually quite normal, and Todd likely was hiding the real reason he wanted out. But she cried herself to sleep every night for months and became obsessed with exercising every morning at five o'clock. She was sure the only way to remedy her pain was to try to look more like a magazine cover.

As a college student I too rode a contentment roller coaster. I had been on occasional dates but had never had anyone to call a boyfriend. I believed that one of two things must be going on: either God was holding out, or there was something wrong with me. I usually dwelt on the latter. I was pretty certain that I couldn't land a guy because of a long list of problems with my appearance. Now I call it the "not-enough syndrome": My hair isn't long enough. My thighs aren't thin enough. My fill-in-the-blank isn't fill-in-the-blank enough. Lots of us have this disease.

During my senior year God decided to address this issue. In my quiet times I was studying the Old Testament, reading it straight through. What struck me in Scripture was unexpected.

The Israelites had been told of the Promised Land when they were in slavery in Egypt, had escaped and had spent forty years wandering in the desert. Now I was getting to the good part. They finally reached their destination and were ready to divide up the long-awaited land.

As I read the account, I imagined a huge assembly of families gathered by clans. Joshua is standing at the microphone, announcing proudly how God told him to assign property. "Benjamites, you get this land over there!" A cheer of celebration can be heard from that gang. "And Judah, you guys get that part of the land!" Another joyous shout, and confetti fills the air.

> ✍ I call it the "not-enough syndrome": My hair isn't long enough. My thighs aren't thin enough. . . . Lots of us have this disease.

But Joshua 13:14 read, "But to the tribe of Levi he gave no inheritance, since the offerings made by fire to the LORD, the God of Israel, are their inheritance, as he promised them." Several times Scripture mentions that the Levites didn't get huge areas of land like everyone else. They got a few towns and some pastureland for their livestock, but the Lord assigned them to live among the people and be priests.

No fair! I thought. *They wandered in the desert and waited not-so-patiently just like everyone else! They are really getting the shaft here,*

God. That was when God spoke more clearly to me than he had ever before.

"Michelle," he said, "I have given the Levites a precious gift of freedom. They don't have to work to care for the land, growing crops and feeding their families. They are freed up to be with me and to have a special calling of ministry. I've been trying to give you this same gift in your singleness, but instead of savoring it you have wasted it."

He was right. Relationships require a lot of work, time and energy. While a dating relationship is what God gives to some, to others he gives singleness. Both are gifts of love. I could not savor God's gift since I thought I was single because of my "not-enoughness." I wasn't gazing at Christ, and my life was plagued with discontent.

I later found that getting married wasn't the solution to my body insecurities anyway. I had assumed that if only I could find Prince Charming to make me feel attractive, my nasty little problem would resolve itself. But my discontent followed me right into marriage. I still felt insecure, because I needed to learn to rest in God's good design for me.

It is a lie that I will be content once I have whatever I crave. Once I have that guy. Once I have those breast implants. Once I get my hair straightened. Those things may put Band-Aids on the problem for a little while. But contentment comes only from relationship with a God who has bigger and better plans for us than we have for ourselves. It comes from a choice to put God in the spotlight.

In what ways has my body been in the spotlight
instead of God's purposes?

FEAR FACTOR

Another consequence of rejecting God's truth about our body is that we live in fear that at any point we can be rejected. We assume everyone shares our critical opinion of our body. We're afraid that not only will we be judged harshly but those around us will ultimately hurt us.

Sometimes we fear rejection from guys. It sounds like a hot talk-show topic, and probably has been: "Men who threaten to leave their wives if they don't lose weight and the wives who . . ." Well, I guess it doesn't really matter who they are as long as they spruce themselves up.

Sometimes we fear rejection from other women. I mean, let's be real. It's other women who notice the details of our appearance—the new shoes we're wearing, the new haircut and whether we've gone down a couple of dress sizes. Most women I know will mention such things within the first thirty seconds of any conversation. We anticipate getting looked over and evaluated.

For the first several years of her marriage, Maria was imprisoned by fear—not so much that her husband would leave her as that he didn't really think she was physically attractive. She hungered for his compliments, but upon hearing them she would sabotage their effect: *He said those things only because that's what husbands are supposed to say, not because he actually meant them.* She felt that she was competing with Hollywood images for her husband's affections: *Surely he thinks they're more beautiful than I am.* She'd sneak glances to catch his reaction to Pamela Anderson and Jennifer Lopez, fearful that she might actually be right. Maria's fear put a damper on their sex life, corroding it like a leaking battery. *What does he really think of my naked body?* She felt guilty, as though her husband had been cheated when he got her as a sexual partner. And she felt ashamed. She was unable to enjoy herself in bed, unable to experience the pleasure and unconditional love God had meant for their marriage.

Song of Songs reveals what Maria was missing. I think of it as God's version of a steamy romance novel, replacing the cheap and cheesy sexual fantasies with the intimacy and safety of marital love. The husband and wife spend the entire book proclaiming their love for one another and delighting in each other's body and soul. They are unconstrained and unashamed.

"How beautiful you are, my darling! Oh, how beautiful!" the lover proclaims. "Your mouth is lovely . . . your neck is . . . built with elegance . . . your two breasts are like two fawns" (not a comparison that particularly speaks to me, but certainly a high compliment in that culture). He goes on, "All beautiful you are, my darling; there is no flaw in you" (Song of Songs 4:1-7).

No flaw? Really? Did this woman actually fit the perfect image of beauty? The truth is that it didn't really matter. Her husband delighted in her body the way it was. No comparisons and no critique.

And I find it interesting that she doesn't argue with him. She allows herself to be cherished and bathes in his expression of love.

There is One who will never reject me.

It is this freedom, this ocean of unconditional love, that God intended for us to know, whether we are married or not. But our fear of rejection drains it dry.

And the harsh reality is that at times others really do make hurtful judgments about our appearance. We women can be quite brutal to one another. Joan and Melissa Rivers have made a career out of their Best and Worst Dressed lists. And unfortunately some guys do consider how a girl looks first in determining whether to pursue getting to know her.

But all too often our assumptions of how others will judge us are just that—assumptions. Not all women are as critical as Joan Rivers. In fact, most of us are more critical of ourselves than we are of others. And not all men are so shallow that mere physical appearance determines their attraction to women. (Those who are like that aren't ready to be in a healthy relationship anyway.)

Marriage counselor John T. Molloy once asked a group of men who had gotten engaged what attracted them to their fiancées when they first met. He recounts,

> Only about 20 percent of those men described their future wives as gorgeous or sexy, whereas more than 60 percent de-

scribed their personalities. That was what attracted most of them in the first place. Even men marrying very beautiful women were more likely to emphasize their fiancée's personality over her physical beauty. . . . I don't mean to understate the effect of physical beauty; there is no question it attracts men. But even when they first meet a woman, it's usually the woman's personality that makes her seem special.

Not only are our assumptions of others' opinions often false, but living in fear of them is a form of slavery that will never lose its grip. We can never fully control the opinions of others. They can only control us. I can never know for sure how someone will respond to me or how they will judge me.

But there is something I *can* know for sure. I can know that there is One who will never reject me. In Song of Songs he calls me his beloved. The fear of rejection places the opinions of other people higher than this One who cherishes me unconditionally. But we must choose whose opinion will really matter to us. Galatians 1:10 prods us to ask, "Am I now trying to win the approval of men, or of God? Or am I trying to please men? If I were still trying to please men, I would not be a servant of Christ."

What things cause me to fear rejection from others
rather than resting in God's unchanging love for me?

PERFECTIONISM AND CONTROL

The list of consequences doesn't stop there. Getting swept up in today's beauty standards sometimes means we will be plagued by the disease of perfectionism. This illness convinces us that we must strive to be perfect in order to be acceptable. If it isn't perfect, then it's horrible. It's all or nothing.

Unfortunately, our culture feeds this tendency. We begin by comparing ourselves to models of female perfection in the media that are virtually impossible to emulate. Yet we are flooded by messages telling us we can have anything we want if we just work hard enough. Loretta LaRoche puts it this way:

> It may be that you simply don't have the body type to be a successful javelin thrower—and you never will. That's all there is to it. But our society says, "Don't limit yourself! If you want to be a javelin thrower, simply work harder at it. Take more javelin-throwing seminars, write goals for yourself, say daily affirmations, and before long, you'll be throwing your way to an Olympic gold medal!"

So we continue measuring ourselves against the "perfect" body, and something in us believes that if we could just get a little closer to this perfection, we wouldn't have to worry about our body anymore.

Karri discovered that her perfectionism had an evil twin sister called control. Growing up in a small town, she had always stood out because of her good looks. She was a cheerleader and homecoming queen, and people often made comments about her beauty. Without even realizing it, she let her identity become wrapped up in her appearance.

When Karri left for college, she was determined to avoid gaining the weight that brought comments from hometown folks. Instead of gaining those famous freshman pounds, Karri worked hard to lose. She kept iron-tight control over everything she ate. No fat. No sugar. Usually she'd eat just a bowl of Grape Nuts and a little bit of broccoli on the side. Karri would tally her calories and make sure to exercise enough to burn off an equal or greater amount of calories each day. She remembers, "I was fanatical about exercising every day for at least an hour. I'd even cancel other things or not visit with friends just to make sure I got in a full workout. My goal was to go to bed hungry. I felt so much satisfaction if I could have enough self-control to avoid food."

After a while Karri began to show signs typical of an eating disorder. She didn't have a period for a year. She started to have digestive problems. Her body even started to grow dark hair all over to help her keep warm, since she had lost the normal layer of protective fat. Despite these symptoms, Karri didn't realize she had a problem until some Christians who cared about her began to intervene.

Our desire to control what others think of us and to control our appearance has led to an epidemic of eating disorders that public health literature has compared to the seriousness of AIDS. Professional counselor Monica Dixon writes,

> I have stared into the hollow eyes of a catatonic young woman who subsisted on half a bagel a day while practicing gymnastics for three hours every day.
>
> I have held the dried and withered hand of a twenty-one-year-old who ran ten miles a day on two bowls of Special K with skim milk.
>
> I have hugged the shaking bodies of young women who drove endlessly from one gas station to another in the middle of the night, buying candy bars, eating them in the car, and throwing them up at the next stop.
>
> I have been awakened in the middle of the night by young women terrified by the seizures of vomiting they brought on themselves by swallowing Ipecac syrup.
>
> I have spoken loudly to university administrators who could not understand why every year they had to put new plumbing in the women's bathrooms adjacent to the dining hall.
>
> I have watched beautiful, bright young women die.

She goes on to cite sobering statistics about our university campuses. "Almost 20 percent of these women are starving themselves to death! Another 50 percent are vomiting their guts out in the university's bathrooms. Many of the 'normal' ones are out running endless circles around the college track, trying to burn up the chicken bouillon they sipped for dinner."

Though our tendencies toward perfectionism may not manifest in eating disorders, the mindset of a perfectionist produces a poison fruit that is deadly in any form. We become caught in a downward spiral that never brings the satisfaction we long for. A perfectionist mindset does not bring freedom from worry but the opposite. Often it propels us full force into body obsessions. In order to keep things perfect we must keep an ongoing account of every little detail. We think, *If they only knew the real me, surely I would be judged harshly.* So we do our best to cover up any flaws that might give us away. We build walls to keep others out.

> ✐ A perfectionist mindset . . . propels us full force into body obsessions.

Chasing perfection is like racing on a treadmill after the proverbial carrot. It only makes us weary, and we never catch our prize. The real irony is that the only remedy is to experience unconditional love. But in order to experience this love, we must let down our guard and expose our flaws. There is delicious freedom in being loved despite imperfection as opposed to "earning" acceptance. Those of us struggling with perfectionism long for the freedom of acceptance but instead end up imprisoned by our own self-protective control.

This is what Karri eventually discovered after a group of Christian friends began to pray for her. One day a staff worker from the campus ministry asked gently, "Do you ever see this part of your life as a sinful area?"

"Huh? What do you mean?" she replied curiously.

"Well, it's vanity. It's idolatry. It's worshiping a certain body type," he stated boldly but still with gentleness.

That's when it clicked. Karri realized that she'd had two idols: her looks and food. Her perfectionism had led her to worship something other than God. She knew the only thing she could do was to acknowledge the sin and come to God, who loves her no matter what.

God began to teach her that the self-control she had been striving for was self-serving, rigid and legalistic. It gave her a sense of power. But the self-control that is a fruit of the Spirit is God-focused, full of grace and seeks "everything in moderation." It brings a sense of freedom.

Karri told me, "I would be lying if I said I didn't struggle still today. But it's different now. If I saw a TV commercial before, it used to make me say, 'Oh, I can't eat tomorrow.' But now I can see that commercial and catch it. I might struggle, but I can say, 'Oh, there it is again,' and take it to God instead."

In what ways am I affected by perfectionism?
How does God need to transform my self-control?

We suffer from believing what our culture tells us about our bodies. We are losing out to discontentment, fear and perfectionism. But this is not God's desire for us. He longs for us to know freedom from these things. We must find a way to let it sink in that God made not only humanity well, but my particular body too. The consequences otherwise are much too costly.

SCRIPTURE TO MEMORIZE

Am I now trying to win the approval of men, or of God? Or am I trying to please men? If I were still trying to please men, I would not be a servant of Christ.
GALATIANS 1:10

QUESTIONS FOR DISCUSSION

1. What kind of conversation do you have with God about the way he made you?

2. What do you think genuine contentment looks like? feels like? How would your life be different if you were content with your body? if you were content with your marital status or future?

3. What is the secret of contentment? How do we develop a lifestyle of contentment like the apostle Paul?

4. How does the fear of rejection affect your relationships with people? How does it affect your feelings about your appearance?

5. In what ways do you feel pressure to look or be perfect?

6. How has God ministered to your fears of rejection or your anxious drive toward perfection?

4 ✑ WHO'S THE FAIREST OF THEM ALL?

Beauty and Ethnicity

BEAUTY IS NOT INSTANTLY AND

INSTINCTIVELY RECOGNIZABLE:

WE MUST BE TRAINED FROM CHILDHOOD

TO MAKE THOSE DISCRIMINATIONS.

✑ *Robin Lakoff and Raquel Scherr,* Face Value

*M*illions of Americans were watching. I was flopped on the couch too, microwave popcorn at my fingertips. A handful of talented young Americans were taking their turn on a television stage in *American Idol.*

Each week show-business hopefuls would perform and stand bravely for critique by three celebrity judges, while viewers phoned in their votes for the best and brightest vocalists. Throughout the series the judges had been clear that being a pop star requires a stellar combination of musical talent and image. Like it or not, in our culture albums sell better if the artist is physically attractive.

It was Kimberley Locke's turn to perform, and she nailed it. Kimberley was a beautiful young woman with a powerful voice. She was also biracial and had a head full of curly African locks. Throughout the series the contestants had been working with stylists to improve their image, and several weeks into the show Kimberley had had her kinky curls straightened. Now her hair was long, sleek and flowing.

After Kimberley sang, the judges responded with compliments and critiques. One of them, a Caucasian male, attempted to compliment her: "Ever since you got rid of that weird hair, you got better!" Immediately I squirmed.

Weird hair? Hair that was dark and kinky and thick—hair that God intentionally designed for millions of people around the world—was *weird?*

Kimberley's radiant smile hid any discomfort the judge's statement may have aroused. But what he said brought to light a serious cultural problem. Many women have discovered an unspoken addendum to the beauty standards of our society: The more European one's features, the more beautiful one is considered to be.

As a white woman, I can never fully understand what women of color experience. But God deeply cares about our skewed notions of beauty, so I do too. Issues of ethnicity make questions about beauty even more complex and sometimes deeply painful.

All women of color do not feel the weight of this problem to the same degree. But here is how Elaine Brown summarizes what she learned even as a young girl: "The rule was simple: The closer to white, the better. We derided girls who had short 'nappy hair,' or 'liver' lips, or protruding, high behinds, or skin 'so black it's blue.' . . . Despite that I was, like most girls on York street, a few shades 'too dark,' I had 'good' hair and white facial features."

BEAUTY'S UGLY HISTORY

Although some have yet to discover it, we live in a highly racialized society—that is, "a society wherein race matters profoundly for dif-

ferences in life experiences, life opportunities, and social relationships." And in a society that tells women we must be beautiful to be
accepted, mixing concepts of beauty
and ethnicity can result in a toxic
cocktail. It's a concoction that's been
brewing for centuries.

Nancy Etcoff has researched the
concept of beauty throughout Western history: "In writings from Plato
onward, the straight profile of the
Greek statue was usually assumed to
be the ideal human face." As history
unfolded, this concept of the Greek
statue as highest beauty permeated European art, philosophy, science
and sociology.

> ✍ His first mistake was beginning with that assumption that the Greek statues were the highest standard for beauty.

In the eighteenth century, Dutch artist and anatomist Petrus Camper
set out to quantify beauty. He invented an instrument to measure the
angles of facial profiles (essentially the incline from chin to forehead)
and designed a system of measurement to compare facial angles across
ethnic groups. His first mistake was beginning with that assumption
that the Greek statues were the highest standard for beauty. Camper
even averred, "We will not find a single person who does not regard the
head of Apollo or Venus as possessing a superior beauty, and who does
not view these heads as infinitely superior to those of the most beautiful men and women."

It's no surprise that Camper's results validated his premise:

Camper thought he had found the angle of beauty. . . . Measuring the skulls of different races, he found that facial angles increased from orangutans and monkeys to African blacks to
[Asians] to the European man and finally to the Greek statue,
making European man the closest to the beauty ideal and African man the furthest.

It would be easy to discount Camper as an eccentric exception to the rule. But unfortunately the same value system permeated European culture, passed on by scientists, philosophers, doctors, farmers, even Christian thinkers.

- In 1907 scientist Edward Angle used his own (European) face as the ideal for producing a classic orthodontic model for straight teeth. By his standard, all nonwhite people would require major orthodontic work to have their teeth "fixed."

- In the 1700s and 1800s American farmers of European descent distinguished their slaves not merely by dark skin color but also by the texture of their hair. Black slaves who had lighter skin and straighter hair—closer to the European standard of beauty—were allowed to work inside the plantation owner's home. This meant labor that was less grueling, as well as access to better clothing, education and food. House slaves also had an opportunity to be freed if their master were to die.

- Camper was not the last to attempt to quantify facial beauty. Later the Swiss-born Johann Caspar Lavater published his own "scientific" findings that Europeans were the most beautiful when he measured facial angles and ordered them from a frog to the Greek statue Apollo. The most appalling fact: Lavater was a *pastor.*

Yes, even God's people were perpetuating a vicious lie. Concepts of beauty were fastened inextricably to racism, and the resulting wounds still run deep.

As European immigrants filled the United States, bringing along the influences from prior centuries, this kind of thinking took root in U.S. culture. We can still see the painful residue of this type of racism.

- A slavery system that gave better work to "whiter" slaves has by now been long abolished, but some women of color find that pursuing a more white appearance (in hairstyle, makeup and clothing style) means greater chances at being hired for a good job.

- Greek statues aren't gracing the covers of magazines as the highest form of beauty, but the few women of color who succeed as models and celebrities still tend to have more European features. Halle Berry and Alicia Keys are certainly good creations of God, but these are the only prototypes of beautiful women of color celebrated by the culture.

- Orthodontics may not be mislabeling nonwhite jawlines as deformed, but sometimes eyeglass companies assume European noses are the norm. My friend Hannah, a Chinese American, was being fitted for glasses but had trouble finding a pair to fit right. The technician tried to commiserate, "Yeah, they don't really make these for flat noses like yours." Later she told me, "I was embarrassed but mad too. Not only did he make me feel like a freak of nature, but I couldn't help but wonder why they don't have my face in mind when they design glasses."

Family life is also affected by the assumption that white is beautiful. One contemporary Latina author writes,

> Our families, often without consciously intending to, pass on a pattern of self-loathing and physical discomfort with regard to our indigenous looks. There are so many nasty names associated with *la india* [Indian]or *la negra* [black], some still so disturbing to me that I refuse to even mention them. It's also sad that our self-loathing has a complex hierarchy, with African on the bottom, Indian next to the bottom, and all the gradations approximating the European ideal ascending from that. . . . These psychologically crippling attitudes have stripped us of our ability to champion, or sometimes even recognize, the beautiful Indian or African women we are.

Naturally some women have found the cultural standards to be more painful than have others. Some have found refuge within the encouragement of their own ethnic community. But others have been greatly affected by racialized beauty standards. Many women fashioned by God to help bear his image are being told otherwise.

After reading about racialized beauty,
how do the facts about our history make you feel?
Angry? Guilty? Helpless? Surprised? Sad?

I believe that God grieves over the tragedy of racialized beauty. Following Jesus means not only having a personal relationship with a holy and loving God but being part of a multiethnic family that cares for one another. It also means that we join God in restoring what he intended for the world. This is a calling for all women, no matter our ethnicity. And we'll never really be able to fulfill this calling unless we understand how racialized beauty standards have affected us *all*. Let's take a look at how women across the ethnic spectrum experience the fallout in different ways.

GOOD HAIR, BAD HAIR

As I've talked with white women about their beauty insecurities, most often the hot button is body size. Bookshelves and infomercials are full of material that is obsessed with weight. As Dyann Logwood notes, however, the key issue is often different for African American women:

> I know Black girls who are comfortable weighing 200 pounds, showing cellulite, and flaunting curves that would send other girls running to the gym. But ask those same sisters to leave the house without their hair done? That's a different story. Few of us are truly at ease with the coarse hair texture that comes courtesy of our African roots. In the beauty spectrum, our natural hair isn't even on the map.

In the black and Latino communities, "good hair" and "bad hair" are labels not for "having a bad hair day" but for how closely one's hair texture resembles the Caucasian beauty standard of smoothly flowing locks. Logwood explains, "In mainstream society, many companies will not even hire us unless we make our hair look like white folks' hair. Many big companies would send us packing if we showed up in a business suit sporting dreads, an afro, or a natural—even though these are natural hairstyles that women can wear without spending money on weaves or perming our hair with potentially harmful chemicals."

The black community has had a long and painful history with hair. Next to skin color, hair texture has been one of the most defining factors used to separate people of African

✍ **"In the beauty spectrum, our natural hair isn't even on the map."**

heritage as racially inferior. Not only were slaves treated differently according to hair type, but for over one hundred years following emancipation, during years of segregation, light-skinned black folks were identified as "Negro" by their hair. Derogatory hair references like "buckwheat" and "nappyhead" were used to insult and tear down.

In the years of the civil rights movement, wearing one's hair "natural" became a strong political statement about black pride. But wearing a natural style often brought harsher treatment. Taylor, a forty-eight-year-old accountant, remembers, "When Afros came out, I wanted to wear an Afro. So I did everything and I finally got me a great big huge Angela Davis Afro. Whenever I would wear my Afro I'd get pulled over by the police."

But wait, there are several black women who have risen to the top of our beauty culture, you may say. What about Tyra Banks and Naomi Campbell, supermodel divas? Notice that such women are hardly ever shown without long cascading tresses, the Caucasian ideal, usually the result of artificial weaves and wigs or hours of expensive chemical processing.

Maintaining hair comes at a high cost. Paying to have one's hair cut, permed (straightened), woven, braided or styled regularly becomes quite expensive. The time it takes to maintain "relaxed" hair can be burdensome! Young girls grow up enduring physically painful routines of combing, styling or chemically treating their hair. In their text *Black Rage,* authors William Grier and Price M. Cobbs argue "that the process of grooming hair is not only painful for black girls, but the end is that black female children look simply acceptable rather than beautiful. One of Grier and Cobb's conclusions is that girls receive the message that their hair in its natural state is undesirable, otherwise they would not have to endure the pain of getting their hair straightened."

> ✍ "I was forced to redefine what made me beautiful."

Sometimes the cost is emotional. Having always worn her hair long and straightened, my friend Lavonne had been curious about what it might be like to "go natural." She even joked with family members about cutting it all off, but they never believed her.

Lavonne graduated from college and secured a job. Now that she didn't have to worry about gaining employment, she realized it was her chance to try what she'd always wondered about. So she naively stepped into a salon and had it cut off. But reality began to set in when her South African stylist started trying to bolster her self-esteem before he was even finished. "You've done a very brave thing today," he said. *What's he talking about? It couldn't be that bad, could it?*

Lavonne paid for the haircut and headed for her car. In her first moments alone, she decided to get a better look at her new style. Gazing back at her from the rear-view mirror was someone she didn't recognize. She recalls, "I'm not joking, I actually screamed out loud." She wasn't prepared for the flood of emotions that would fill up the car that day. "My standard of beauty had been one thing my whole life [longer straight hair], and now that was gone. I immediately wanted to put on some earrings or something that would make me feel feminine."

Questions raced through her head. *Am I still beautiful? Will I be mistaken for something I'm not—lesbian, political activist, angry black woman? And now what do I do with it? Gel it? Braid it? I don't know anything about hair products or how to care for it. Will my family think I've lost it?*

She called home to break the news. "Look, Mom, I'm coming over, and I have an Afro. So just don't flip out."

Changing to a natural hairstyle began for Lavonne as a naive act of curiosity. But the Lord used it to teach her some valuable things about herself. What did she value? Whose opinions would she listen to? Now that she didn't fit the description of beauty she'd assumed for so long, Lavonne mused, "I was forced to redefine what made me beautiful."

Sometimes women experience difficult consequences of a hyphenated ethnicity in a racialized society.

DOUBLE STANDARDS, DOUBLE TROUBLE

San Juan, Puerto Rico, is a beautiful place full of beautiful people. When I went to live there the year after graduation from college, I encountered a number of cultural surprises, but what really caught me off guard was the first time one of the sweet older women affectionately called me "gordita," which translated literally means "little fat one." It was meant as a term of endearment, but to a white girl from Illinois it sounded like a huge insult. Back home most women I had known would rather die than be called fat. It took awhile to get used to the cheerful Puerto Rican use of the term.

So what happens for women whose heritage has a different beauty standard from that of *Cosmo*? Sometimes women experience difficult consequences of a hyphenated ethnicity in a racialized society: Korean-American. Mexican-American. Japanese-American. Filipina-American. Cuban-American. One culture uses one measuring stick while the "louder" dominant culture uses a polar opposite system of measurement. The result? Confusion. Frustration. Insecurity. If a woman is acceptable in one context, she may not be acceptable in the other. She is pulled in two different directions.

When Sandra was growing up, her family encouraged her to keep plenty of meat on her bones.

> To be a *flaca* [thin] Latina was to grow up feeling *fea* [ugly]. Women . . . wore tight jeans and spandex to enhance their big butts, and the men loved it. I remember my pride at being complimented for having *piernas gordas* [fat legs] like my mother! . . . I got to college and discovered . . . that strange world outside of my barrio and family suddenly stripped my chunkiness and my rotund derriere of their attractiveness. Unfortunately, it was my first time away from home, and my desire to fit in was so intense that instead of questioning these new cultural standards, I adopted them as my own—I started a war against my "big" butt and thighs. And it made me feel schizophrenic; too *flaca* in the barrio and too *gorda* downtown.

Latinas aren't the only women affected by double standards. As I've talked with young Asian American women, I've discovered that many of them experience the same tension in reverse. Julia, a nineteen-year-old Chinese American, remembers,

> I grew up surrounded by Barbie dolls and magazine cover girls like actresses Alicia Silverstone and Cameron Diaz; they were my main examples of beauty. . . . I also grew up with another set of standards that went hand in hand with the common stereotypes of Asian women. I discovered that, as Asian American

girls, we are supposed to be short, lightweight, petite, soft-spoken, and light-skinned, with long, straight, jet-black hair. . . . Unfortunately, my parents believe that I will not catch a nice (hopefully, Chinese) boy to marry me if I weigh over 120 pounds and wear anything larger than a size 8.

Ellen too has felt the tension of double standards. She once told me, "In the U.S. I am comparatively too small, too short, too flat-chested. But when my aunts come to visit from Hong Kong, they comment on how fat I am. They say, 'You know, even the XL size in China would be too small for you.' My mother even jokes with me that I must have East Mountain Canyon blood in me—they are a people group in northern China that are known to be large."

THE EYE OF THE BEHOLDER
While living between two worlds with differing beauty standards, some Asian American women struggle with specific physical features. Shin An, a Korean hairstylist, recalls, "Growing up among the blonde, blue-eyed girls of Kenosha, WI, I permed my hair and even considered getting eyelid surgery to look 'more Western.' Once on a trip to Korea, in my early 20's, I tried using a cosmetic glue pen meant to create a temporary crease that mimics an upper eyelid. It was a disaster! My lashes got stuck in the glue, and I looked truly scary!"

Plastic surgery among young Asian women is on the rise.

Often women of Asian heritage are complimented for having big, round eyes with a distinct fold in the eyelids—double eyes, as Lois-Ann Yamanaka calls them. Sitting in a plastic surgeon's office, waiting while her sister looks into getting plastic surgery on her eyelids, Lois-Ann recounts what it was like to be Japanese American growing up in Hawaii. She remembers longing for the eyes of the white girls who were movie stars.

We would get those eyes by stretching and pulling and then taping and gluing the skin of our lids back into a self-made fold. . . . And then we'd have haole eyes. No more Oriental eyes . . . slant eyes, seeing-through-venetian-blinds eyes, kamikaze eyes, your-ancestors-started-World-War-II eyes, Nip eyes. We had double eyes, thank you very much, even if we couldn't wet our faces when we went to the beach, lest we emerge, eyelids sagging, glue white and bumpy, and pieces of Scotch tape floating like shiny dead minnows in the tide.

Glancing across the surgeon's office, Lois-Ann watches her sister. "The look she gives me makes me sad. In her eyes, I see all the Asian girls and women who have mutilated themselves in the hopes of looking white."

Though taping and gluing don't seem to be as common as they used to be, plastic surgery among young Asian women is on the rise. Western television has influenced women overseas to seek a more European look. A friend has told me that in Korea plastic surgery is so common that when a young woman is engaged to be married, her future in-laws will sometimes request photos from early childhood to see her physical features before any alterations were made, revealing what genes she will actually pass on to their grandchildren.

Take some time to journal about some women you know.
What are their burdens in the beauty culture?
What about women of other ethnicities you don't yet know?
Ask God to heal your own body image issues in the
process of becoming other-centered.

❧

DYING FOR ACCEPTANCE

The sad truth is that we haven't even scratched the surface of the various ways that ethnocentric beauty standards play out. The list goes on and on. Some African, Asian and Latina women get the message that their noses are too flat. Some Jewish and Italian women are told their noses are too big and unfeminine. Middle Eastern women can struggle with the connotations of dark facial hair. And across the board, women of color most often find that when it comes to skin tone, the lighter the better.

Grace's five-year-old came home in tears because she wasn't "pretty" like the blond, blue-eyed girls at school.

Some women of biracial or multiracial heritage find that their physical appearance is a source of confusion for others; this can breed feelings of shame or frustration in them. Many feel that there is something wrong with them, that they never fully fit in anywhere. I spoke with a young woman whose father is Italian and mother is Venezuelan. Elena told me, "I remember the trauma of the locker room in junior high. Getting undressed with everyone only emphasized the ways I was different. I always thought something was wrong with me because their nipples were pink but mine were brown. It wasn't until years later when I saw Halle Berry topless in a movie that I had a revelation. *She has brown nipples! I'm not alone! There is nothing wrong with me!*"

I wonder how Elena's journey might have been different had she seen more examples of beauty in the media that look like her. Now don't worry, I'm not suggesting we be given more opportunities to see Halle Berry in the buff. But with so few nonwhite images of beauty visible in advertising, television, magazines and movies, the lie of ethnocentric beauty only gets reinforced.

Asian American women have been virtually invisible within mainstream beauty culture. My Korean American friend Grace told me that her five-year-old came home in tears from kindergarten because she wasn't "pretty" like the blond, blue-eyed girls at school. Grace took her daughter to the store in hopes of buying a beautiful new dolly that would have Korean features. But not surprisingly, she couldn't find one. I cried with my friend that day as we thought about the painful message her precious daughter had already begun to internalize.

Here's a challenge:
take a minute to jot down names of women of color who
are considered beautiful in our culture.
How long is your list?

With such negative messages, it may be no surprise that eating disorders are on the rise among women of color. Once eating disorders were thought to be mainly a white-culture problem, but this life-threatening crisis has spread among people of other ethnicities. *Essence* magazine surveyed its readers about overuse of laxatives and diet pills and about starvation. Compared to a similar survey by *Glamour* magazine, the results showed that in every category black women revealed more difficulties than white women did—a reflection of the struggles women of color face. Another integrated study surveyed nine hundred middle-school girls, ages eleven to fourteen, and found that Latina girls reported higher levels of body dissatisfaction than any other group and were at higher risk for eating disorders. I have also found article after article journaling young Asian American women's struggles with anorexia and bulimia.

Even in Fiji, where weight gain was once a sign of health and beauty, Harvard researchers have discovered a surge of eating disorders and dangerous dieting among girls since the introduction of Western television in 1995. Racialized beauty standards are more than traumatic: they can be life-threatening.

DARK AND LOVELY

Song of Songs tells the story of a woman who doesn't fit the beauty standards of her time either. But even though some reject her, she remains confident and secure. Their opinion doesn't really matter, for she knows her Maker made her well.

> Dark am I, yet lovely,
>> O daughters of Jerusalem,
>> dark like the tents of Kedar,
>> like the tent curtains of Solomon.
> Do not stare at me because I am dark,
>> because I am darkened by the sun.
> My mother's sons were angry with me
>> and made me take care of the vineyards;
>> my own vineyard I have neglected. (Song of Songs 1:5-6)

According to Bible commentators, either the "daughters of Jerusalem" make up part of King Solomon's harem or this is a generic reference to upper-class young women of the day. Either way, this group of women seems to be judging our young bride for her dark skin. Probably her skin tone is not necessarily an indicator of her ethnicity but of socioeconomic class, since she tells us that the sun is to blame. Wealthy women, especially those belonging to the king's harem, were usually put through beauty treatments that were expensive and extensive, sometimes lasting for months or years. Often they included treatments to lighten the skin. Working-class women, on the other hand, would be exposed to the sun regularly as they labored outdoors. Thus even in ancient Israel skin tone was used to judge some as inferior.

🖋 Even in ancient Israel skin tone was used to judge some as inferior.

Our bride acknowledges fully that she doesn't fit the beauty standard. She knows that she has "neglected her own vineyard." She knows that in the eyes of the daughters of Jerusalem, their staring eyes, her dark skin renders her unattractive. But her tone is not defeated. It's as though she is saying, "Yes, I am dark. Really dark. Maybe darker than anyone you've seen. I don't fit your description of what makes a girl attractive. But listen to me: *I am lovely.*"

She is unaffected by the stares and judgment because she knows it is not their opinion that defines her. She has confidence that she is created beautiful, and the other characters in the play confirm that this is true. Friends respond in verse 8 by calling her "most beautiful of women." And her lover spends the rest of the book gushing over her beauty. He calls her beautiful or lovely thirteen times and goes on to admire each body part.

She does not need her culture to validate her attractiveness. She knows she is beautiful just the way she is, and those closest to her confirm it.

Our bodies are not a mistake. None of us. In fact, the Bible says, "You were bought at a price" (1 Corinthians 6:20), and Jesus did not purchase any of our bodies from the clearance rack. Psalm 139 tells us that we were "knit together" by God just the way we are. Our ethnic heritage. Our family likenesses. Our body.

> God tells us in his Word that he knit us together. With excitement. With hope. With joy. And with precision.

I don't know how to knit. But my friend Mimi does, and I've watched her in action. Mimi begins with a vision of something beautiful. She chooses her yarns carefully, taking into account the colors, the textures, the quantity. At any moment in the process if you ask her what she is making, she beams with excitement and hope as she describes the finished product she envisions. She gestures as if modeling the garment that is still in her mind's eye:

"Can't you just imagine how cute this will be?" Her project usually requires hundreds, if not thousands, of individual twists of yarn. She is attentive to each one, and if a single stitch isn't quite right, she'll undo the row and start again.

God tells us in his Word that *he knit us together*. With excitement. With hope. With joy. And with precision. It is the evil one that would have us believe differently.

Process how you feel about your own ethnicity.
God chose it for you in love.
Ask God to speak to you about how he knit you together.

I think this is why the bride in Song of Songs was able to shut out the voices of the daughters of Jerusalem. She knew that God had knit her together with precision. She didn't fit her culture's criteria of beauty, but she was able to proclaim with confidence, "I am lovely." She was wonderfully made.

Some of us need to dwell on that a while.

Some women don't fit the Eurocentric standards and need to hear God say, "I knit you together. You are wonderfully made." We need to ask God to make us more like the bride in Song of Songs.

Others of us have features that are "acceptable." We may feel guilty as we see how other women are hurting, or we may feel uncomfortable when others gush over us and compliment us. We may need to wrestle with the same truth: we are knit together too. We are no more and no less wonderfully made. And sometimes the ones spilling the compliments may need to hear that just as much as we do.

Maybe the starting point for all of us, women of every ethnicity, is to identify where we have blindly bought into the standards of beauty that are ethnocentric. *What have I defined as beautiful to the ex-*

clusion of other features? What might God have to say to me about the way I am knit together? about the ways other women are knit together?

How can I be more like the woman in *Song of Songs*? What is God asking me to do next? How can I be an encouragement to women of other ethnicities? We need to have some honest dialogue with God and with other women about these things.

Lavonne turned toward the mirror, spread her arms and said, "Sometimes you just got to say, 'I love myself!'"

For some women, a next step may be to get rid of beauty rituals that perpetuate the lie that whiter is better. Remember my friend Lavonne, who got her hair cut off? She had relied on long, straight hair to make her feel beautiful, to fit in with mainstream culture. But when she found herself without it, God began to reshape her definition of beautiful.

Currently Lavonne has a particular ministry in my life: helping me understand that God made me beautiful. She exudes confidence and contentment with her own body, and she is always teaching me to be the same. Not long ago we were standing in front of a full-length mirror, shooting the breeze about this and that. Lavonne turned toward the mirror, spread her arms and said, "Sometimes you just got to say, 'I love myself!'" Then she had me do the same.

I admit I felt a little silly. But I realized that Lavonne is a gift in my life to help me digest God's truth about my body. Even if I have to be force-fed occasionally.

Lavonne confided that cutting her hair allowed God to do something in her family she never expected. It opened up a whole new intimacy in her relationship with her parents. They began to talk about their past experiences with hair, which led to reminiscences about racial injustice and the civil rights era they had lived through. These were stories they had never told her before.

It seems God was eager to bring great blessing to Lavonne as she learned to live outside the culture's ethnocentric beauty standard. And she has become a blessing to other woman as a result. She is able to affirm all kinds of beauty in others, because God has freed her from a limited image of what is beautiful.

Everyone doesn't have to do what Lavonne did. It's not wrong for women of color to choose certain beauty practices associated with a European heritage. But let's all pay attention to the not-so-subtle cultural messages that those are the only acceptable forms of beauty. And sometimes we learn deep things from God when we are willing to shake things up a bit.

Such a complex and painful issue has no simple solution. If women of various ethnicities got together to discuss possible solutions and ask God what is the next step for us, I wonder what might happen. Might God bring greater contentment and confidence? Might he root deeper in us the truth about his good design of our bodies? Might he bring healing? Might he even lead us into greater intimacy and honesty with others? Are we willing to find out?

SHARING THE BURDEN

When I began to explore the lives of women of color and what they experience in the beauty culture, I quickly realized that I had underestimated their journey. It's a journey that I may never fully understand or appreciate. Yet it is a journey that I can join.

We have a lot to teach each other. It is our ethnic isolation that keeps us from learning from wise women. Some of my most treasured friendships, those that have taken me farthest on my journey of healthy body image, are with women of other ethnicities. I need them. And they need each other. Grace's Korean American perspective is healing for Lavonne, and Lavonne's African American perspective is healing for Elena. These friends need me too: the perspective I offer is different from some of the messages they've heard from white culture. By God's grace, my stories and my love for them might be vehicles of healing as well. God's design for multiethnic community is truly for our good.

Frankly, without multiethnic relationships our view of the world remains flat and one-dimensional, especially for white women. We are impoverished without women of color. My friend Rita spent several months living with a small village of Afro-Colombian people in rural South America. During her stay she painted portraits of people she met, as a way of honoring them and telling their stories. Rita spent hours examining the details of their faces and features while building relationships with each of them. She explained, "The beauty of an Afro-descendant person is no longer theoretical for me, not just a piece of my theology. In my heart's symbolic language, white features are no longer the standard, normal or automatic. The world teems with more beauty than ever before, and I am all the richer."

> ✍ Unless we are in relationship with women of other ethnicities who are experiencing pain different from our own, we will never care enough to do something about it.

In addition, we will never know about injustices perpetuated by racialized beauty standards unless we are in relationship with women who are experiencing them. But when we know and affirm one another, we can drown out the voices of the ethnocentric beauty culture. We need to hear each other's stories. We need to get hurt with each other and get angry at what our sisters in Christ experience. Unless we are in relationship with women of other ethnicities who are experiencing pain different from our own, we will never care enough to do something about it.

God calls his children of all ethnicities to join with one another in their pain and struggle. The apostle Paul isn't subtle: "Carry each other's burdens, and in this way you will fulfill the law of Christ" (Galatians 6:2).

One of the things I liked about being pregnant was that people liked to help me "carry my burden." Even complete strangers would respond. It made me feel special, loved and not alone. I will never forget the time I was eight months pregnant, my burdened belly bulging, and was at a garden center looking at birdbaths with my mom. As I bent over to inspect the one my mother had decided on, another customer came leaping across the perennials to my aid. "Don't move that!" she yelled. "Let me do that for you. I would hate to see you go into premature labor."

So how do we carry the burdens of others? First we must recognize the burden. We do that by asking questions about their experiences. We listen, really listen, to the things on their heart. Often deep feelings are expressed not directly but subtly.

Then we enter the burden with them, imagining what it would be like to be in their shoes. Carrying one another's burdens means that we become "other-centered." Often this is just the kind of step *we* need: to get our eyes off our own body problems and experience healing from body-image sin caused by self-absorption.

> ✍ Our compassion must turn to practical action. How can I serve you? How can I communicate that you are beautiful? How can I defend you?

But it doesn't end there. Had the woman in the garden center merely thought, *Wow, it must be tough to be in her place,* she would not have picked up the birdbath. Our compassion must turn to practical action. How can I serve you? How can I communicate that you are beautiful? How can I defend you? Maybe it's through an encouraging word. Maybe through prayer. Maybe by taking a stand against injustice when we see it.

One of the benefits of living in a capitalist society is that money has power. What we choose to do with our money can have far-reaching effects, especially if we join forces with like-minded women who want to see racialized beauty standards changed. Sandra Guzman writes, "Since the birth of Hollywood, magazines and mainstream media have rendered us invisible or portrayed only those [of us] whose looks matched the Anglo ideal: long, straight dark hair, thin features, and a svelte body. . . . The fact is, it's hard to control media representations, though we *can* influence them by using or withholding our buying power." We can decide not to purchase products from companies that are offending women of color, whether blatantly or subtly. One friend of mine has decided not to shop at a certain department store until they include women of color in the photos of models in their displays; she has written the company to let them know.

There will also be opportunities to speak justly. When we notice ethnocentric beauty standards, whether in advertising, while shopping at the mall or in conversation with others, we can speak up. We can write letters, send e-mails. We can point out ethnocentric thinking in others when we hear it. Certainly we must speak in love, maybe even with a bit of gentle humor. Confrontation does not necessarily mean speaking harshly. But to remain silent is to allow God's children to continue getting hurt.

Some of us are in a season of making major life choices: where to live, where to work, where to worship, who to spend time with. Say I am considering a career in business. Where could I work that would allow me to battle ethnocentric beauty standards? Maybe my position would give me influence over who gets hired. How would I change expectations about job seekers' appearance? Say I'm planning to teach. What will I teach young girls about multiethnic beauty? Maybe I'm thinking about moving. Where could I live that would not be ethnically isolating?

Pray and journal:
What is a next step for me in building deep
and affirming multiethnic relationships?
What might God be asking me to do to fight for justice?

George Washington Carver once said, "When you do the common things of life in an uncommon way, you will command the attention of the world." Imagine what God might do in the world if we learned to carry each other's burdens and take a few steps toward building a world that celebrates the unique ways God has made us each beautiful.

SCRIPTURE TO MEMORIZE

Carry each other's burdens, and in this way you will fulfill the law of Christ.
GALATIANS 6:2

QUESTIONS FOR DISCUSSION

1. What are some evidences of ethnocentric beauty standards that you have either experienced or witnessed?

2. What stories or facts struck you most in this chapter? Why? How do you think God feels about these things?

3. How closely do you relate to the young woman in Song of Songs? What would it take for you to respond to beauty standards with the same confidence?

4. What have you been processing alone with God about how he knit you together?

5. What are some ways you can carry the burdens of other women affected by racialized beauty standards?

5 ☙ WHO ARE WE TRYING TO PLEASE?

Beauty and Sin

AS SOON AS BEAUTY IS SOUGHT NOT FROM

RELIGION AND LOVE, BUT FOR PLEASURE,

IT DEGRADES THE SEEKER.

☙ Ralph Waldo Emerson

I can't quite remember when I first realized that I had issues with my body. But I can identify the day I crossed the threshold of womanhood. It was the first time I experienced the trauma of buying a swimming suit.

I was thirteen years old, and our family was leaving for a vacation to Hawaii. This, of course, required new beach attire. My mom and I checked the racks at the department store, and I chose several suits that would surely help me turn the heads of any cute male tourists my age. Then we headed into the fitting room.

The first one I tried was rather anticlimactic. *That's strange. It looked so adorable on the hanger.* As I put on the suits one by one, my disappointment mounted. Each made me feel worse than the last. I pounded my fists on the outer sides of my thighs. "If only I didn't have these!" The morning ended in tears and the purchase of the first of many swimsuits that made me feel rotten about my body.

My body-image issues continued to surface periodically. Throughout high school I was aware of the feeling that I wasn't as pretty as the other girls. During college I knew that it probably wasn't healthy to blame my appearance for my lack of boyfriends. In my twenties I would constantly compare myself to the seemingly flawless women I saw on TV.

But all along, though I was aware of an unhealthy pattern, I merely put it under the category of "issue." An "issue" was what my friends and I affectionately called anything that caused tension in life—like my issue with always losing my car keys, my issue with roommates who didn't pass on phone messages, my issue with walnuts. I had plenty of "issues." This was just another of them.

But one day I stumbled upon a passage of Scripture that revealed to me this wasn't just an "issue." It was ugly *sin*. Sin as offensive to God as adultery, greed, pride and betrayal.

FAIRY TALE OR FACT?

Ezekiel was a twentysomething guy who grew up in the Jewish religious world, most likely the son of a priest. When the king of Babylon, Nebuchadnezzar, captured Jerusalem, Ezekiel and many other Jews were exiled. The people of Israel not only were scattered from one another but also grew distant from God. By the time Ezekiel was about thirty years old, the Lord began to speak to him about the spiritual state of Israel, messages that he wrote down over the next few decades while he spoke his prophecies. God wanted the Jews to wake up and acknowledge the ways they had rejected their Lord.

Often God's message of rebuke came through Ezekiel in the form of a story or metaphor. Ezekiel 16 weaves a tale of a young girl (meant to represent the people of Israel) who has rejected the one who loves her most. Certainly the vision was given to Ezekiel to address the rebellion of the Jews. But I believe it also has relevance to young women today.

God's vision to Ezekiel begins when the girl is an infant, rejected and neglected by those who should have cared for her.

> On the day you were born your cord was not cut, nor were you washed with water to make you clean, nor were you rubbed with salt or wrapped in cloths. No one looked on you with pity or had compassion enough to do any of these things for you. Rather, you were thrown out into the open field, for on the day you were born you were despised. (Ezekiel 16:4-5)

This girl is doomed to die. Born into a harsh and broken world, she is helpless on her own to change her death sentence. But God has compassion on her. He saves her life and takes her into his home.

> Then I passed by and saw you kicking about in your blood, and as you lay there in your blood I said to you, "Live!" I made you grow like a plant of the field. You grew up and developed and became the most beautiful of jewels. Your breasts were formed and your hair grew, you who were naked and bare. (vv. 6-7)

Is the story sounding familiar so far? Those of us who have experienced Jesus' saving grace remember the feeling of being headed toward death. We too were helpless in a harsh and broken world. And we have fallen in love with a God who went searching for us, who swooped in to save us from our own death sentence and has taken us into his home. He has nourished us, healed us and helped us to grow into women who reflect his beauty.

This is a picture of a God who adores us. It is a God who is deeply in love with us.

> Later I passed by, and when I looked at you and saw that you were old enough for love, I spread the corner of my garment over you and covered your nakedness. I gave you my solemn oath and entered into a covenant with you, declares the Sovereign LORD, and you became mine. (v. 8)

It's a fulfillment of the romantic dreams that we women are so obsessed with. Reality TV is making millions off shows that involve people finding their perfect match and falling in love—well, supposedly. Turn on The Learning Channel and you'll find endless episodes of *The Dating Story* and *The Wedding Story*, followed by *The Baby Story*— none of which could happen, presumably, without a preceding Makeover Story. (What do you think we're "learning" from that?) Christian fiction is filled with our church version of love connections. We long to find perfect romantic love—to be cherished, pursued, adored. In Ezekiel, God reveals his intentions to sweep us off our feet with such intense love that we pledge "to love and to cherish" one another the rest of our days.

The story goes on to tell of God's love for the girl and his lavish care for her.

> I bathed you with water and washed the blood from you and put ointments on you. I clothed you with an embroidered dress and put leather sandals on you. I dressed you in fine linen and covered you with costly garments. I adorned you with jewelry: I put bracelets on your arms and a necklace around your neck, and I put a ring on your nose, earrings on your ears and a beau-

tiful crown on your head. So you were adorned with gold and silver; your clothes were of fine linen and costly fabric and embroidered cloth. Your food was fine flour, honey and olive oil. You became very beautiful and rose to be a queen. And your fame spread among the nations on account of your beauty, because the splendor I had given you made your beauty perfect, declares the Sovereign LORD. (vv. 9-14)

God spared no expense in making us who we are today. From the moment we began a relationship with him, the Holy Spirit has been in a process of transforming us into perfection. Part of God's purpose for me daily is to mold me, refine me and make me into a head-turning beauty.

This is also true of our physical bodies. As the story recounts, God chooses the finest materials, foods and jewelry to make this girl into a beauty queen. He has done the same for us. The hair he gave me is a beautiful crown. My arms, my neck, my nose and my ears—they are like precious jewels. My skin type and body shape are woven together like the costliest fabric. My genes are nourished to fruition by culinary delicacies. God is impassioned when he declares, "The splendor I had given you made your beauty perfect."

Let that sink in. No, really. Do we believe it? God drew on his own splendor to create my body. Every single part was chosen for me from the most priceless of treasures—including the parts I would rather trade in for a better model. And when God steps back to look at the full picture, he deems my beauty perfect.

✒ God drew on his own splendor to create my body. Every single part was chosen for me from the most priceless of treasures—including the parts I would rather trade in for a better model.

What is my response to reading God's words,
"The splendor I had given you made your beauty perfect"?

LOOKER OR HOOKER?

You might think this girl has it made. Since being saved from death, she has been flooded with extravagant love. No expense has been spared to make her exquisite. She is so beautiful that she has become famous. One might think she'd be a model of contentment. Surely she would be secure and confident in God's love.

But here is where Ezekiel hits us with the kicker. God says,

> But you trusted in your beauty and used your fame to become a prostitute. You lavished your favors on anyone who passed by and your beauty became his. You took some of your garments to make gaudy high places, where you carried on your prostitution. Such things should not happen, nor should they ever occur. You also took the fine jewelry I gave you, the jewelry made of my gold and silver, and you made for yourself male idols and engaged in prostitution with them. And you took your embroidered clothes to put on them, and you offered my oil and incense before them. Also the food I provided for you— the fine flour, olive oil and honey I gave you to eat—you offered as a fragrant incense before them. That is what happened, declares the Sovereign LORD. (vv. 15-19)

I was curled up on the overstuffed chair in my living room when the Holy Spirit nailed me. One word kept leaping off the pages of that leather-bound book. *Prostitute.* You used your beauty to become a *prostitute.* You took the priceless jewels I used to adorn your body and offered them in *prostitution.* I had that funny, heavy feeling in my stomach that I get when the Lord has a word of conviction for me.

What? A prostitute? Not me. Don't you think that's a little harsh, Lord?

I wrestled with God over it. *There is no way. Maybe I'm a little unhealthy. Maybe I need to deal with my issues. But a prostitute?*

Then God flexed his muscles. This was no "issue" in my life. It was ugly sin—sin as raw and audacious as prostitution.

> ✐ We all know that in our society beauty is power.

A prostitute uses her body to gain a profit. How often I have attempted to use my appearance to gain approval from others. I have taken the body that God created out of treasure and used it as currency in exchange for love, power, esteem and a long list of desired commodities.

Let's just be honest. We all know that in our society beauty is power. The "beautiful ones" get noticed, get favored and get better treatment. A recent psychology study asked seventy-five college men to look through photographs of women whose physical attractiveness varied. They were asked to choose those women for whom they would be most likely to do the following: help move furniture, loan money, donate blood, donate a kidney, swim one mile to rescue her, save her from a burning building or jump on a terrorist hand grenade. Not surprisingly, the men overwhelmingly chose the most beautiful women in every case, being reluctant only to loan her money.

Being considered beautiful can mean not only better treatment but also emotional gain. There is a twisted sense of power we feel when we can make someone notice us. I remember struggling with this when I was dating. I felt powerful if I could make a guy desire me by dressing attractively. I realized I could use my body to get a reaction.

To be clear, within a healthy marriage relationship there is nothing wrong with delighting in one another physically. A husband and wife's bodies are gifts to one another, and getting dressed up for your loved one can be a very appropriate way to communicate love. But there is a twisted version of this that is about seeking power rather than expressing selfless love. There can be a puffed-up sense of affirmation when we get noticed for our appearance. The days that I "look good," hair done and sporting trendy clothing, I have more confidence. In my hunger for love and acceptance, it is tempting to use my body as currency to win people over.

Some of us have a wardrobe that could be considered to be stocked with lethal weapons. Our clothes cling to every curve, waistline exposed, cleavage accentuated, rear end practically waving hello to anyone who might glance its way. Some of us may not be quite so obvious, but our intentions in investing heavily in our appearance are the same. We long for attention, for affirmation, for the power of being considered beautiful. Just like the prostitute, we use our body to gain a profit.

How do I use my beauty to gain a profit?

A prostitute is someone who is desperate. Certainly no one turns to this career for the status. Most often these women are fighting for survival: a runaway teen who finds that the street is no place to live; an unemployed single mother searching for a way to feed her kids; a young woman sold into prostitution in order to pay off family debt. No hope for income. No hope for freedom. No hope for alternatives.

When I use my appearance to gain the approval of others, I have taken desperate measures to fill a hole. I have become convinced that there is no other alternative. I believe that there is no other way to feel secure, affirmed and valuable. Like a hungry lion on the prowl, I am starving for love because I have fasted from divine affection.

But this is foolishness. God offers the very thing we long for—in abundance. Our girl in Ezekiel had more than she could have ever asked for: extravagant love, an extravagant life. God builds her a home of safety, acceptance, adoration and affirmation. How foolish she is to turn away from the Lover of her soul in search of a substitute. Just like Ezekiel's prostitute, how foolish I am in my desperate desires.

What have I become desperate for that might cause me to prostitute my beauty?

A prostitute forgoes exclusive intimacy and gives herself to anyone willing. This is not the Julia Roberts-Richard Gere kind of fairy-tale prostitution pictured in the movie *Pretty Woman*. Girlfriend in Ezekiel is not awaiting her true love to whisk her away in a limo like a knight coming for his princess. This is a tragic story of betrayal. Instead of savoring her exclusive intimacy with God, she gives her body to "anyone who passed by and [her] beauty became his" (Ezekiel 16:15). Later in the passage God says to her, "You adulterous wife! You prefer strangers to your own husband!" (v. 32).

The pain of betrayal is clear in God's voice. What were meant as gifts for his cherished wife were pawned off to others. "You also took the fine jewelry *I gave you* . . . and engaged in prostitution *with them*. And you took your embroidered clothes to put on them, and you offered *my* oil and incense *before them*. Also the food *I provided* for you—the fine flour, olive oil and honey I gave you to eat—you offered as fragrant incense *before them*" (vv. 17-19).

I am starving for love because I have fasted from divine affection.

I too have betrayed God by giving myself to anyone passing by. I have preferred the acceptance of strangers over God's lavish love for me. When I get dressed in the morning, I dress for *them*. When I wear a swimsuit, I'm embarrassed to be seen by *them*—or I flaunt myself for *them*. When I feel disappointed at the reflection in the mirror, I have given ownership of my beauty to *them*. When I tell myself that I feel ugly today, it is because I care more about what *they* must think of me than about how God sees me. Who are *they*? My culture, my friends, the opposite sex, the general public. Anyone passing by.

In *Eve's Revenge*, Lilian Calles Barger muses on how we live conscious of the fact that the world is gazing at our bodies and judging them. So much of our stress comes from our perceptions of what people must be thinking when they gaze at us.

> ✍ I care more about what *they* must think of me than about how God sees me. Who are *they*? My culture, my friends, the opposite sex, the general public. Anyone passing by.

> Because we expect to be looked at, because we have internalized that phenomenon, we have formalized the gaze and created various rituals around it: fashion shows, cheerleading, the Miss America pageant, the elaborate wedding ceremony in which any woman can be Miss America for a day. . . . After a lifetime of living under the gaze, one day you realize that you are getting older and any beauty that you had or hoped for is fading. Younger men no longer look at you. Older men are too busy gazing at younger women. But instead of feeling relief, many of us experience this as though our security blanket had been taken away. We are afraid that we will not be able to keep the man we have or get the man we hope for. . . . Whether you are unscathed or not, you continue to accept the tyranny of the gaze because you have been trained from childhood to submit to it and dance before it.

Ezekiel was showing me that I'd been dancing before *their* gaze,

hoping that it might end up the way it did for Julia Roberts's character. The red gown and happily ever after. If I could find acceptance
from those I perceived to be gazing at me, I would certainly know
contentment and happiness. But the reality is that I have given away
to strangers what I should be saving for God. He is the One I have
pledged myself to. My beauty belongs to him. He gave it to me. It is
meant for his good pleasure—the pleasure of an artist gazing at his
masterpiece or a husband gazing at his wife. Instead I've sold it.

How am I betraying God when
I strive for the affections of others?

℘

OUR TWISTED URGE

Why would it be so tempting to betray our marriage with God for a
life of prostitution? Quite possibly the temptation is rooted in a fatal
flaw that began the moment sin entered the world. God warned us
that the result of our sin would be to hunger for acceptance from
men. His words to Eve in the garden foretold it: "Your desire will be
for your husband, and he will rule over you" (Genesis 3:16).

The relationships between men and women have become a
twisted version of what God originally intended. Remember Adam
and Eve in the beginning? Living in a lush garden, contented and
loved. Carefree. Accepted. But when they chose rebellion over relationship with God, their Maker spelled out the consequences of
their decision. Just like Eve, women would be bent toward an unhealthy desire to find acceptance from men; and men, like Adam,
would have a sinful urge in their nature to control and dominate.
Derek Kidner explains,

> The phrase *your desire shall be for your husband* (RSV), with the re-
> ciprocating *he shall rule over you,* portrays a marriage relation in

which control has slipped from the fully personal realm to that of instinctive urges passive and active. "To love and to cherish" becomes "To desire and to dominate." While even pagan marriage can rise far above this, the pull of sin is always towards it.

Barger puts it this way:

Yearning to recover the one-flesh union she had with man in Eden, woman will place man in the position reserved for God, looking to him for fulfillment. Instead of unity, woman will find that the man often becomes her emotional and physical master. Her exercise of power is centered on pleasing or manipulating the man (most readily evident in the use of sexuality), which in turn enslaves her more.

While we were created to desire God, the sinful urge was born in women to instead desire men. We deceive ourselves into believing that a husband will satisfy the cravings of our soul. So we look for that knight in shining armor who will give us our happily ever after. Mary Ellen Ashcroft calls this the "white knight syndrome." She recalls meeting a college student who was a textbook case: "Only eighteen, Karen has carefully learned the catechism taught to her by the world in the church. 'What is the highest calling of a woman?' Unlike the church catechism that would lead her to reply, 'To glorify God and enjoy him forever,' Karen has learned the world's version: 'To serve a man and make him happy forever.'" As a result, Karen expects the man to "fill center stage in her life," a distorted relationship that amounts to idolatry.

Unfortunately this is a pretty unfair expectation. How in the world are men supposed to do for us what God was meant to do? Clearly they can't. In my single days I used to think that the remedy for the white knight syndrome was to get married. While marrying my husband ended my days of waiting for that special someone, it didn't take away my twisted urge to find fulfillment in him.

I looked to him to make me feel loved, to keep me from loneliness, to make me happy when I wasn't, to give me wise advice, to help me grow spiritually . . . the list went on. And while those things are often benefits of a healthy relationship, God did not put him in my life to fulfill my needs. Otherwise I wouldn't need God anymore. I also found that my husband didn't make a very good Lord of lords.

At first I got frustrated with him. He wasn't meeting my needs. He wasn't fulfilling his husbandly duties. Then God reminded me that my expectations for him were unfair. Of course he couldn't do for me what only God could do. I needed to let go of desire to be filled by my husband and replace it with desire for God.

Unfortunately men have a sinful urge as well that only feeds the problem. This is the other side of the gender dysfunction coin: the urge to dominate, conquer and control. In this mindset, women can become objects—very often sexual objects. It's no wonder that pornography has such a powerful draw. Images that objectify women's beauty are tempting. Thus the barrage of media images—images feeding obsession with women's bodies and culturally defined beauty—gains momentum. Women see those images and believe we must look like them in order to land that perfect guy who will fulfill every need.

God did not put my husband in my life to fulfill my needs. Otherwise I wouldn't need God anymore.

Our twisted urges feed off one another like a warped game of Ring-Around-the-Rosy. We all fall down. Until we women replace our desire for men with a desire for God, we will remain susceptible to the habit of investing heavily in our appearance in hopes that it will buy us the affection we crave.

THE PERFECT MATE

Beauty carries with it an empty promise of the perfect love relationship. If I am attractive enough, my prince will come. We use our body as bait for Mr. Right. And once we have caught him, we must keep him interested. So we are compelled to keep chasing after the impossible beauty standards of our culture. But our unrealistic expectations for men to fulfill us only lead to disappointment. Men will fail. They can't possibly fill the shoes of our perfect mate, the One who calls himself our heavenly bridegroom.

> ✑ We use our body as bait for Mr. Right.

I wish Jenny had figured that out. When she joined our fellowship on campus, she stood out like a polished gem. She was friendly and energetic. Her bubbly personality was like a magnet. She was hungry to grow spiritually and was serious about her relationship with Jesus. And she was adorable. Great clothes. Cute figure. Bright smile.

Jenny was on the fast track toward leadership in our group. She was everything we look for in a potential leader. She was gifted, driven and committed. I started meeting with her regularly, and we talked about real-life stuff—Jesus, classes, guys. Jenny was also a dancer. Fitness was crucially important, and she was very self-critical of her body. She always had to look just right, and like many of us she struggled to find contentment in the way God made her.

It wasn't long before Jenny was swept off her feet by Mr. Fraternity Guy. He was fun and good-looking and had grown up in the church. He seemed really great. But my time with Jenny began to be monopolized by two topics. One was the pressure to be physically perfect; the other was her dating life. One day I asked Jenny what she thought God might want to do in her future. She responded without hesitation, "Oh I don't know, I just want to be a wife someday."

Certainly the desire to be married is not a bad one. But her response was symptomatic of the fatal error we women tend to make. We substitute a relationship with a man for our marriage to God. Jenny became less interested in serving Jesus and more interested in *Bride* magazine and what to wear to the formal. She'd originally had

_✐_ **My Maker is my husband. I don't need to use my body to gain affection. I don't need to be considered beautiful to be affirmed.**

a desire to do inner-city work, but that quietly faded into the background now in favor of her new leading man.

Several years later I caught up with Jenny. She was married and was involved in her church, but something was missing in her. It was as though a spark had been snuffed out. I often wonder where Jenny would be with God, how she might have blossomed, what incredible places God might have taken her if she hadn't allowed a guy to take center stage in her life.

It's no misprint that God calls himself Israel's husband. In fact he tells his followers that they will know more joy than someone who has a husband and children.

> Sing, O barren woman,
>   you who never bore a child;
> burst into song, shout for joy,
>   you who were never in labor;
> because more are the children of the desolate woman
>   than of her who has a husband,
>   says the LORD. . . .
> Do not be afraid; you will not suffer shame.
>   Do not fear disgrace; you will not be humiliated.
> You will forget the shame of your youth
>   and remember no more the reproach of your widowhood.
> For your Maker is your husband—
>   the LORD Almighty is his name. (Isaiah 54:1, 4-5)

My Maker is my husband. I don't need to use my body to gain affection. I don't need to be considered beautiful to be affirmed. I am already married to the One who made me, who loves me like no one else, who considers me exquisite and who promises me great joy through intimacy with him.

How do I need to grow in living as though God is my husband?

THE CROSS

It never feels good to discover sin in our life. In fact it's something we'd much rather hide and pretend we never noticed.

When I was little, my parents gave me Flintstone vitamins every morning with breakfast. The only problem was that I didn't like the green ones. I found them particularly gross. I wasn't one for open rebellion, so it never crossed my mind to tell my folks I didn't want to eat them. And I thought for sure that if I threw them in the trash, my mom would find them there when she began to empty it. So I devised a brilliant plan. Each time I got a green vitamin, I would put it in one of two clever hiding spots: in the couch cushions or in the Kleenex box.

Unfortunately I hadn't thought my plan all the way through. On a cleaning day my parents found the stash in the couch, and it never occurred to me that eventually the Kleenex box would be empty, so that Mom would discover a cardboard percussion instrument with green vitamins rattling around inside.

Sometimes we would rather try to find a clever hiding spot for our sin when it surfaces than deal with the problem. Especially when God might be comparing our sin to prostitution. But it's as futile as Flintstone vitamins in the Kleenex box. The sin will just keep coming back to haunt us.

The good news is that convicting us of sin is only the first half of the Holy Spirit's job. After he has made us aware of sin, God offers us forgiveness and a way to live differently. Jesus told us, "When [the Spirit] comes, he will convict the world of guilt in regard to sin and righteousness and judgment" (John 16:8). But he also said, "The Counselor, the Holy Spirit, whom the Father will send in my name, will teach you all things and will remind you of everything I have said to you . . . for he lives with you and will be in you" (John 14:26, 17). The Holy Spirit doesn't just show us the ugly junk and then leave us hanging. His job is to lead us to freedom and make us new. Titus 3:5 says, "He saved us through the washing of rebirth and *renewal by the Holy Spirit,* whom he poured out on us generously through Jesus Christ our Savior."

Take some time and talk to God right now about how you'd like him to make you new.

L♥

This was exactly what the Holy Ghost was doing for me the day I read Ezekiel. He made it clear that using beauty to gain affirmation is unacceptable. God needed an apology from me, so I confessed to him that this "issue" in my life was much like the sin of prostitution. I asked him to take away my bent toward a sinful body image and make me new.

I still have an "issue" with losing my car keys, but I'm grateful we have a God who doesn't leave us to wallow in the messes that we create when we choose sin over his good and perfect plan for us.

SCRIPTURE TO MEMORIZE

Since you died with Christ to the basic principles of this world, why, as though you still belonged to it, do you submit to its rules?
COLOSSIANS 2:20

QUESTIONS FOR DISCUSSION

1. Look back at the story in Ezekiel. Has God rescued you from death in a broken and harsh world? Explain your answer.

2. What parts of Ezekiel's story were most striking to you? Why?

3. How do you respond to the analogy of prostitution?

4. How have you experienced the urge to desire after men instead of desiring after God? How has that urge affected the way you feel about your body?

5. What do you need to confess as sin? How do you want God to make you new?

6 ☙ CAN I STILL KEEP
MY FAVORITE LIPSTICK?

Beauty and Balance

BEAUTY IS NOT ON THE FACE;

BEAUTY IS A LIGHT IN THE HEART.

☙ *Kahill Gibran, Lebanese poet*

I would love to look in a mirror someday and be able to be happy with what I see," said Kelly tearfully. "I want to be able to look at my appearance and feel good about who I am."

Rachel could relate. She said quietly, "I feel average because I look at myself in a mirror and that's what I see." Later she added, "I want to make a difference in my life. I don't want to feel sorry for myself."

Many of us have had these feelings, while some of us simply fear the possibility of looking unattractive. We're tired of feeling the way we do about ourselves, but it seems there are few alternatives in life. Kelly and Rachel both decided that the only way out was radical plastic surgery. Both became contestants on the reality TV show *The Swan*. Each week two women would undergo major reconstructive surgery, and cameras would follow their three-month recovery process. At the end of each episode, one of the two women would be chosen to participate in a beauty pageant and possibly be crowned queen.

Producers of the show claimed that it was supposed to "inspire" plain Janes, because "anybody can be a *Swan*." But critics found the tone of the show rather disturbing and called it "ghastly." Some questioned the message it sent to women who don't measure up to cultural beauty standards. Some questioned the message it sent about plastic surgery in general. With contestants undergoing as many as twenty procedures, the surgery was actually quite dangerous. Ronald Moy, president of the American Society of Dermatological Surgeons, said, "These shows create the perception that a patient's appearance can be changed radically without risk. Risk in surgery goes up with multiple procedures and time under general anesthesia." A few astute

> ✍ I don't want social beauty pressures to consume me, but does that mean I have to get rid of my lipstick?

critics noticed the holes in the *Swan* philosophy of life improvement, when women who have been surgically altered are told that they're still not quite good enough to win a beauty pageant.

Nevertheless, it appears that the entertainment industry might be onto something. The Fox network claims that ten million viewers tuned in to watch *The Swan*. And TV shows like it have become increasingly popular: *Extreme Makeover* (where makeovers are surgical instead of just a new haircut and makeup), MTV's *I Want a Famous Face* (where people get plastic surgery to make them look like their favorite celebrity) or melodramas like *Nip/Tuck* (about the world of plastic surgeons). Could it be that our society has resolved that the only way to escape the pressure to look a certain way is to slice and dice our bodies?

I mean, what's the alternative? Forsake beauty products altogether, move to Antarctica and wear a cardboard box? Or is it time for us women to rally, staging massive bonfires to cleanse ourselves of our hair extensions and nail polish? I can just imagine compacts and hair dryers being hurled into the inferno. Journalist Katie Couric stands by interviewing impassioned participants. "Heads up, Katie! Incoming *Buns of Steel* video!" they yell. Behind them someone is being hauled away on an ambulance gurney after an unfortunate nose-piercing mixup.

There must be a middle ground. Before we decide to declare war on beauty, we must first decipher where to draw the line. Do I wave the white flag, giving up and giving in to the culture's solution of plastic surgery? Or do I swing the other way and declare beauty products my enemy? I don't want social beauty pressures to consume me, but does that mean I have to get rid of my lipstick? Somewhere there has to be a healthy balance.

BALANCING ACT

Trying to define what balance looks like is a bit tricky. It seems that a balanced response to the beauty culture isn't a black-and-white yes-or-no stance. Think of a continuum between two extremes: body obsession and body neglect. A balanced response avoids both ends.

Anything we do because we're focused on what others think of our appearance or because we want to prove we're worth something could be termed *body obsession*. Such behaviors are motivated by pride, fear, shame or control. Body obsessions are rooted in the heart, travel to the mind and bear fruit in our actions.

Ashley wouldn't have called herself a slave to fashion, but getting dressed each morning was quite an ordeal. Standing in front of the closet in her towel, she went into mental gyrations. *Let's see. Who will I see today? Oh, Karen and Rebecca would be so impressed with that shirt. But if I wear those jeans with it, I'll be worried about my butt all day. If only I had some cute red sandals. That would make me feel so much better.* Ashley's struggle began with insecure fears that her coworkers would either affirm or judge her based on her apparel. It traveled to her thought life, which was riddled with self-conscious questions. And it bore fruit in the choices she made each day about her wardrobe.

It isn't that boot-cut jeans or strappy red sandals are intrinsically good or bad. The problem begins long before the choice to wear those things. Anything can be the result of a body obsession: doing our nails, straightening our hair, counting calories or shopping for new clothes. We can be obsessed with certain rituals, like putting on lipstick, or we can be obsessed with specific body parts, like the shape of our eyes or how flat our tummy is (or is not). To identify body obsessions, we must ask ourselves, *Does this behavior express worry about my appearance? Is it based on fear of what others think of me? Does it drive me to focus too much on impressing others instead of resting in God's love for me? Has it been occupying an inordinate amount of my time? my money? my thoughts? my conversations?* Asking these questions may help us to identify what needs to change for us to take our focus off our body and return it to God's truth and God's priorities.

✐ Anything we do because we're focused on what others think of our appearance or because we want to prove we're worth something could be termed body obsession.

On the other hand, *body neglect* would manifest in any behaviors that hurt my body or in any failure to take care of it. Often such neglect results from shame, control, laziness or an overly busy lifestyle. It can even reflect a misguided idea that taking care of our bodies is not spiritual, that those who love Jesus are not concerned with their physical selves.

If our bodies are gifts from God, then we are to steward them well. Brushing my teeth is taking care of my body. If I don't, my teeth will rot. Cleansing my skin is taking care of my body. If I don't, my skin will clog with dirt and oils, bacteria will grow, and pores will become infected. (A slightly more biological way of saying "I'll get zits.") Getting regular haircuts—whether stylish and hip or not particularly so—helps my hair to remain strong and healthy. Eating wholesome food is taking care of my body. If I don't pay attention to nutrition, or if I eat for reasons other than hunger and nourishment, I am neglecting my body's needs. God designed our bodies to need motion and exercise as well. We think better, grow stronger, breathe better and function better when we get plenty of movement. In fact, obesity and physical inactivity can lead to diabetes, heart disease, cancer, osteoporosis and tooth decay.

There is a whole list of things we sometimes leave out that help take care of our bodies: wearing sunscreen, using conditioner, drinking water. One could even argue that pedicures are healthy for our feet. Some of us do fine with personal hygiene, but embarrassment about our body shape has led us to avoid clothing ourselves appropriately. We hate to go shopping—it brings up our body insecurities—so we avoid fashion altogether. Body neglect happens when we fail to do things to take care of ourselves or when we do things that end up harming our bodies.

Body neglect would manifest in any behaviors that hurt my body or any failure to take care of it.

Still, defining balance is a bit tricky. Some behaviors may even fall on *both* ends of the continuum. I would suggest that a desire for plastic surgery is rooted in body obsession. We are convinced that the only way to find contentment and happiness is to permanently change the parts of our bodies that upset us. It becomes so important to us that we are willing to spend thousands of dollars on a solution that doesn't address the underlying issue. And plastic surgery actually ends up as an expression of body neglect. The very procedures we subject our bodies to in hopes of finding contentment can be quite dangerous and invasive. People have died from surgery that involves cutting, slicing, adding foreign objects or removing an entire section of the body. This is damaging one's body, not caring for it.

Eating disorders would also fall at both ends of the spectrum. There are various types of eating disorders, and each of them can be triggered by any in a long list of catalysts—abuse, pressure, failures, fears, family dysfunctions. Though they may be triggered by different things, often eating disorders express a body obsession. Fear of becoming fat. Fear of being out of control. Focusing on body size and beauty routines to an extreme. But eating disorders also result in a type of body neglect. Though the intention may be to "take care" of the body, the result is actually extremely harmful. The body goes into starvation mode. It can't nourish itself. It can't keep warm. Whole organ systems begin to malfunction, potentially bringing heart failure, digestive problems, hair loss, shutdown of the reproductive system. And overexercising only magnifies the problems. The behaviors of eating disorders are actually destroying the body.

I wish I could say that I have found the secret to staying balanced 100 percent of the time. But unfortunately, the truth is that it is a daily struggle to keep my intentions in check. We are complex beings. I

A balanced response to the beauty culture requires that I come before God daily—maybe even minute by minute—and ask him to show me when my behaviors manifest body obsessions and when they reflect body neglect.

might be doing just fine with my approach to wearing makeup or cleansing my skin but at the same time be making poor choices about eating or be incredibly self-conscious because I've got the wrong socks on today. The reality is that living a balanced response to the beauty culture requires that I come before God daily—maybe even minute by minute—and ask him to show me when my behaviors manifest body obsessions and when they reflect body neglect. It requires that I pull back and allow God to transform the way I treat my body in general. It requires some hard reflection and some tough decisions, but I think Scripture offers some guidelines that will help us.

Where do I fall on the balance continuum regarding my body? How about food? exercise? fashion? grooming? specific body parts?

Body obsession ——————————————————— Body neglect

✍

HOLY CONTAINERS

Mary Kay Ash, founder of Mary Kay Cosmetics, once said, "Balance doesn't just happen. To achieve it we must first establish our priorities." Some of the most helpful guidelines to establishing balance and priorities come from a guy who was criticized for having an unimpressive appearance, the apostle Paul.

The church in Corinth was having some major problems with sexual ethics, and Paul chose to address the problem by teaching the Corinthians about their bodies. Their bodies weren't just physical shells separate from their spiritual life. Their bodies were actually holy containers with priceless contents. He wrote to these believers, "Do you not know that your body is a temple of the Holy Spirit, who is in you, whom you have received from God? You are not your own; you were bought at a price. Therefore honor God with your body" (1 Corinthians 6:19-20).

Our bodies are actually temples. Maybe you've heard this phrase thrown around before. Paul used the metaphor of a temple to indicate some notable characteristics. The temple was significant in worship. It was a holy place. Everything about the temple was constructed to point people to God. More than an ordinary structure, it was decorated with ornate and costly features. Nothing was allowed that might lead someone to worship something other than God. And the temple was where the King of kings dwelled. This was the residence of divine royalty. Like a great royal palace, it was treated with dignity, respect and awe.

Take the temple Solomon built in Jerusalem. It was massive and awe-inspiring. Statues and carvings of cherubim were placed all around, reminding the people of the "protective and overshadowing wings of God." Some think that these creatures were depicted as praising God, that their feet were poised to fight off evil or even that God's Spirit sat enthroned upon them. Regardless, they helped temple dwellers to encounter God and worship him. Other symbols were used for the same purpose: palm trees, flowers and pomegranates. Possibly these symbolized the Garden of Eden, helping worshipers to know that they could make things right again with God through sacrifice and atonement.

Growing up in white evangelical churches in the United States, I had little understanding of how a building could affect my worship experience. The purpose of a church building in this culture is mainly to be a meeting place. In fact, it usually reflects what we appreciate about our relationship with God: that Jesus can become our friend. We are moved by the fact that we can be casual with God. We don't have to dress a certain way or say certain words or be formal with him. I can just be me. Many of our buildings reflect that value—carpeted floors, couches in the lobby, chairs in the sanctuary, sometimes even theater seating. Walls are hung with art or bulletin boards or Bible verses in calligraphy. The building is supposed to be comfortable, inviting and functional, mostly containing things we would have in our own home. There are toys in the nursery, silk flower arrangements by the altar, a full-service kitchen, and a pop machine in the youth room. Worshipers come wearing whatever is comfortable—skirts, khakis, jeans. Just be yourself.

Then I went to Russia.

During that visit we had a chance to visit an Orthodox church and worship there. To be honest, my attitude going in was rather condescending. *These poor people,* I thought. *How sad that they don't know Jesus wants a personal friendship with them.* I wasn't expecting to get a lesson in worship.

The outside of the building made the unmistakable statement that this was an Orthodox church. The five massive teardrop structures on the roof proclaimed its purpose from miles away. Upon entering the building, I was given a scarf to cover my head in submission to a holy God. The floors were made of beautiful marble, and there were no chairs. Everyone stood through the hours of the service in honor of God. Every surface within the sanctuary was covered in precious metals and intricate carvings of Bible stories. I could not enter that building without knowing for certain that God is holy, awesome and enthroned in power and authority. It captured my full attention.

> ✒ Has it ever occurred to us that the way we treat our body can be a statement to the world about who God is?

While both places of worship reflect some spiritual truths about God, it wasn't until my experience in Russia that I realized the importance of the building for worship. Far too often I am able to enter a worship service at my own church without truly reflecting on who God is. This may be part of what Paul was referencing when he said our bodies are temples of the Holy Spirit. The temple actually gave people an experience of an all-powerful God who wants to make it possible to know him intimately.

Has it ever occurred to us that the way we treat our body can be a statement to the world about who God is? The way we dress, the way we eat, the way we recreate, the way we care for our body—even the way we talk about our body—can all point people to Jesus.

This can be a helpful guideline for us as we seek a balanced response to the beauty culture. Does my behavior point to God? For some of us, taking care of our hair—getting it trimmed, washing and styling it regularly, even adorning it with clips or jewelry—can be actions of taking care of our body in order to steward it well. Such choices say, in effect, "God, you gave me this body, and you live in it, so I am going to treat it well." But for others of us, the very same behaviors are about bringing glory to ourselves. We do those things to receive attention or affirmation from others. We need the Holy Spirit to help us discern whether the way we treat the Holy Spirit's temple points to God or to ourselves.

What behaviors are the result of inviting others to worship my appearance instead of worshiping God?

No Distractions

In the same way, we need to be cautious that the way we treat our body is not distracting others from noticing Jesus in our life. Sometimes the way we choose to dress becomes a distraction in our "temple," inviting others to worship our body instead of allowing God to receive his due worship. I suggest that the best way to avoid this is modesty.

Modesty is a word that has gotten a bad rap. You're probably fighting off images of rocking-chair grandmothers buttoned up to their chins or naive church ladies spouting religious rules. But it simply refers to the decision to treat your body with respect and avoid inviting others to worship it. Modesty is defined as a freedom from conceit or vanity that results in appropriate dress, speech and conduct.

It seems that modesty is hard to find these days. Our world is all about self-indulgence and self-promotion, and these values have taken over the fashion industry. A collegiate columnist writes, "As soon as the weather reaches the low 60's, college girls seem compelled to throw off their sweaters for shirts that look like swimsuit tops and lay aside their pants for shorts that look like underwear. If it is not really that hot outside, what truly motivates girls to immediately dress so scantily?" I think most of us know the answer to that one. It turns heads. It feels good when people gaze at us.

 I recently learned about a principle used within the advertising world. According to the Gestalt theory, the human brain is able to fill in what is missing from a picture with just a few small cues. We are wired to automatically complete images. For example, look at this diagram. Technically it's a picture of five circles, each missing a sliver. But what do you notice? The brain automatically completes the image, doesn't it?

The same becomes true as we present our body in the clothing we have chosen. The less modest our clothing, the more we invite others to fill in the blanks and complete the picture of our naked body. Although God intended us to be sexual creatures, our body was meant to be a gift, a reservoir of pleasure to be enjoyed within the safety and beauty of marriage. In Song of Songs 4:12, the man says of his fiancée, "You are a garden locked up, my sister, my bride; you are a spring enclosed, a sealed fountain." Until the point of marriage, we don't need to open our body to anyone else's gaze. It would be like carrying delicious chocolates as a special gift for someone but letting anyone I meet along the way sample the delicacies. If it's a precious gift, I'll save it for the lucky one it was meant for.

Dannah Gresh puts it this way:

> Again and again, the Bible reconfirms that this intoxication is only to be shared with one guy . . . and after you're married. . . . Until then, the fullest secrets of the incredible masterpiece

of your body are to be your unique secret. As you might have noticed, some girls aren't the best secret keepers. They flaunt their bodies in hip huggers complemented by belly rings, miniskirts matched to high heels, tight shirts to go with tighter pants and . . . well I could go on.

Does this mean I have to hide my body in a burlap sack? Of course not. Modesty doesn't mean that I can't be fashionable. But there are plenty of stylish clothing options that don't cause my body, my temple, to become a distraction for others.

Sometimes we need friends to help us notice when we've crossed a line of modesty. My friend Melissa tells me that she used to be fairly clueless about the way her immodest choices could be a distraction.

Once during college she met with a guy friend to plan a Bible study. About twenty minutes into the planning time, Melissa was excitedly

> *The less modest our clothing, the more we invite others to fill in the blanks and complete the picture of our naked body.*

spouting off the things she'd observed in the Scripture passage. "Jesus was so compassionate! I love that about him, he—"

Her friend stopped her midsentence. "Can I ask you something?"

"Of course," Melissa said, surprised.

"Ummm, well," he said hesitantly, "would you mind buttoning your shirt one button higher?"

Melissa's face quickly matched the print of the red-letter edition they were reading. "Ooooh! I'm so sorry!"

She felt really embarrassed, but she was grateful that her friend had had the courage to say something. However difficult it was for him, he taught Melissa about the line of modesty. We need to be willing to do that for one another. We don't have to give up fashion altogether, but modest choices will help us to live a balanced response to the beauty culture.

Are some items in my wardrobe distractions in God's temple?
Who can J ask to help me analyze the modesty of my clothing?

SMASHING IDOLS

Sometimes in order to find balance, we need to acknowledge that some of our beauty rituals have become like idols in the temple, causing us to be self-focused instead of God-focused. For the Jews, an idol was a tangible object that caused them to worship something other than the Lord. Though they went often to the temple and it pointed them toward the one true God, it seems they regularly let other things have their affection. "The people of Judah have done evil in my eyes, declares the LORD. They have set up their detestable idols in the house that bears my Name and have defiled it" (Jeremiah 7:30).

Centuries earlier, when Moses was up on a mountain getting the scoop from God about how to set up the Israelites' tabernacle to worship him, the people got this crazy idea to hand over their jewelry, melt it down to make a calf and worship it instead. Yep. That's right. They chose a cow over the Almighty God. Now I grew up in the midst of Midwestern farmland, and trust me when I say this was a bad choice. All cows do is eat, moo and stink. I'd love to know whose brainchild this one was. "Hey Aaron, I've got a great idea. While your brother is off negotiating with the Creator of the universe, the One who flung stars into space and split the Red Sea, let's destroy our expensive jewelry and worship a walking hamburger." Brilliant.

Sometimes we are just as foolish. We may not pray to a life-size poster of the Revlon CEO, but we easily allow tangible things from the beauty culture to become idols that sneak in and defile our temple. Most of the things themselves aren't inherently evil, but we've become addicted to them because they make us feel secure and acceptable. They are stumbling blocks that cause us to fall headfirst into body obsessions. That lipstick I can't be seen without. The jeans that enhance my behind. Those magazines that keep whispering lies. My curling (or straightening) iron that makes me acceptable. They are things that can sabotage our efforts to be a temple for a holy and loving God. It may be helpful to us to give them up for a short time, or maybe get rid of them permanently.

I had no idea how many things had become idols in my temple until I had to go without them for a while. Three weeks after I gave birth to our third child, our family was in a car accident, and an inflated airbag broke my right arm. Unfortunately I am right-handed, so I couldn't do much of anything while it was immobilized in a cast.

In the weeks that followed, I had a lot of help from loved ones. But my normal beauty rituals went out the window. Someone else had to wash my hair. I couldn't blow-dry it. Or curl it. As a lefty, I was pretty inept. When I tried to put on makeup with my left hand, I looked more like a clown than anything else. So I gave up on the makeup. And right after one has a baby, clothes don't fit right for a while. Not to mention that a giant cast isn't exactly the most fashionable accessory. Bozo with stringy hair and a saggy belly. Mmmm-hmmm. I was feeling attractive.

The first few days were torture. I felt so self-conscious about my appearance that I wanted to hide. I thought for sure people who saw me would be thinking, *Yuck. I can't believe she looks so bad.* They'd feel sorry for me. I kept thinking, *I'm so embarrassed. I wish I didn't look this way.*

But I didn't really have a choice: I had been sentenced to six weeks in that lovely cast. So I began to talk with God about the way I was feeling. "Lord, this stinks! I feel so ugly like this."

Slowly I began to hear the words of my loving heavenly Father. "My precious child. You don't need those things to be valuable. Your beauty goes beyond mascara and hair dryers and designer jeans. Be confident in my love for you."

God's gentle words to me had new meaning. Though I would have said I believed those things before then, his truth became like a new pair of glasses with which to see. I could either face the world with fear, assuming people were thinking the worst of me, or I could face the world knowing that their opinion didn't really matter. After a while my self-consciousness began to melt away.

Once my cast came off and my wrist improved from therapy, I was able to dry my hair and apply mascara again. But having fasted from those things for a while had allowed God to break through. When I couldn't use beauty rituals as a crutch, I realized how those things had become idols. They encouraged me to worship beauty—to believe I was valuable only if I was made up. I'd been leaning on those things to feel secure. It was actually freeing to be without them and find a new source of confidence and security. God knew it wasn't just my wrist that needed healing.

> *When I couldn't use beauty rituals as a crutch, I realized how those things had become idols.*

The change in my heart became evident after my cast was removed. From the middle of my hand to a few inches above my wrist, a renegade patch of hair had begun to grow. The "normal" wrist on the left arm appeared smooth, the only body hair so fine and light that it was practically invisible. But on my right I had morphed into freak gorilla woman. It was like my own little grassy knoll dividing the highway of hand and arm.

Before my "fast" from beauty rituals, I would have flipped. I would have been consumed with self-consciousness, immediately mapping out a plan for efficient but painless hair removal. But instead I just chuckled a bit and had some fun showing it off and cracking jokes about my future as a circus act. My physical therapist said it was the result of a stimulated immune system and something about my skin. But I knew it was another opportunity to either listen to God's truths or give in to my fears of what other people thought of me.

Sometimes the best way to discover balance, to uncover things that have become body obsessions or body neglect, is to fast from things that we have come to depend on. Maybe our idol has been buying expensive fashion labels. Maybe it's counting fat grams. Maybe it's makeup or hairstyles. Maybe our idols are magazines or TV shows. Giving them up for a while may help to reorient our priorities. It may give God opportunity to show us things in ourselves we didn't realize were there. It may help us to hear God's truth about our body in a way that requires immediate practical application. It may help us recognize the line of balanced beauty.

What do I need to fast from?
What products or rituals have become idols that God may be asking me to give up for a while?

THE ROYAL TREATMENT

The temple was a special place because it was where God's Spirit dwelled. It was the palace that was home to the King of all kings. It was decorated with precious stones and the most valuable of materials. I imagine it would have put the Ritz Carlton to shame.

King David knew that a temple for the Lord required the best. He said with satisfaction, "With all my resources I have provided for the temple of my God—gold for the gold work, silver for the silver, bronze for the bronze, iron for the iron and wood for the wood, as well as onyx for the settings, turquoise, stones of various colors, and all kinds of fine stone and marble—all of these in large quantities" (1 Chronicles 29:2).

According to Paul's words, our bodies too house the Lord of the universe. Therefore our temples require the royal treatment. God de-

serves to dwell in a temple that is clean, healthy, cared for, with dec-
orations fit for a king.

Many beauty products and rituals have nothing to do with the ac-
tual health of our body. What about makeup, or highlights, or nail
polish, or a really cute dress? When we rid ourselves of the desire to
use these things to gain approval from others, using them can actually be a way of delighting in the body God gave us. It can be a way
of decorating the temple for the royalty residing there.

For many of us such things have become devoid of sacred signifi-
cance. Food has become either addiction or enemy. Exercise is a
torture regimen invented by the beauty industry. Fashion is just a way
to win the approval of others. Body piercing and tattoos are about "self-
expression." Brushing my teeth is merely mundane. Nail polish and highlights are just superficial. But Kristen knew differently.

> *✍* Using beauty products can actually be a way of decorating the temple for the royalty residing there.

She showed up at our retreat with a basketful of nail polish and hair dye packed in her suitcase. She called it her female bonding supplies. I immediately wrote it off as superficial girly stuff that I wasn't really interested in. After all, isn't coloring your hair and nails for the vain females?

As I got to know Kristen, I realized that she didn't have a vain bone
in her body. She couldn't care less what others thought of her appearance. She had a peaceful confidence that came from knowing she was
a precious daughter of the living God. But she seemed to take joy in
pampering her body. Kristen loved to play around with different fashion statements. One day an urban look. The next an eclectic collection from the corner resale shop. Kristen's hair was guaranteed to be
a different color every time I saw her, including bright pink or lime
green. And when she sorted through that basket of nail polish, her
face lit up like a little girl's on Christmas morning.

It seemed a paradox. *Someone content with her body who loves beauty products? How could it be?* Then I realized Kristen understood that her body is the residence of royalty. She took joy in embellishing it. Her desire to color her hair wasn't driven by cultural values. It wasn't about impressing anyone or living up to a certain beauty standard. She simply knew that her body was a gift from God and that it delights him when we enjoy his good gifts. She knew her body was a home to the Holy Spirit, and she loved hosting him. She said, "You hang pictures and light candles in your house. Why not have fun decorating your body?"

Karen Lee-Thorp and Cynthia Hicks, authors of *Why Beauty Matters*, express it this way: "Calls to ignore our outer appearance as spiritually irrelevant do not help us. Quite the contrary: the more we honor our bodies as us, as intertwined with our spirits, as limbs of Christ, temples of the Spirit, and bearers of God's image, the more we will understand and manage well the power of physical appearance in our lives."

It made me wonder about the where I draw the lines of balance. Could shopping for clothes be a way of cherishing my body instead of a means to fit in? Could stepping on the scale be a matter of making my temple healthy instead of comparing myself to supermodels? Could washing my hair, cleansing my skin, wearing sunscreen, eating salads, even wearing nail polish all be ways to extend lavish hospitality on the Holy Spirit who resides within my body?

I think the apostle Paul would say, "Yes! Now you're getting it! Treat your body with respect, giving it what it deserves, the way you would if you were hosting God himself in your home. Don't you realize that your physical body is the dwelling place of the King of kings? Treat it that way!"

*In what ways do I need to be a better host to the
Holy Spirit who lives in my temple?*

FINDING THE BALANCE

When we are living a balanced response to the beauty culture, we don't need to surgically alter our body, but we don't need to throw out beauty products altogether either. In fact, when our motives and intentions are right before God, I would suggest that using some of these things can be a way of honoring him and caring for the body that is his temple. Living in balance means that I can take care of my body by pampering myself, but I'm not tied to those routines. I have freedom to wear makeup and perfume, but I don't get flustered if I'm going out for lunch "unprimped" in a T-shirt and baseball hat. I have the freedom to get a manicure, but it won't bother me if my nail polish is chipping when I have guests over. I can be careful to eat healthy foods, but I can still enjoy the occasional hot-fudge sundae.

> ✒ It is Jesus who must shine his light of truth into the dark corners of our heart and help us find the balance.

There is a thin line between worshiping idols and joyfully engaging in beauty rituals as a way to take care of our body. But somewhere near that line lies the answer to whether or not I need to get rid of my favorite tube of lipstick.

The Holy Ghost must draw this line for us. Getting a manicure might be the fruit of buying into the lies of our beauty culture. God may want manicures thrown out of the temple for a while. Or a manicure may be a way to take good care of my holy container. Losing weight may be an idol for me, the result of loathing the body my perfect Creator has made. Or it may be the kind of commitment I need to make in order to make my temple a healthy one. It is Jesus who must shine his light of truth into the dark corners of our heart and help us find the balance.

In *Eve's Revenge,* Lilian Calles Barger writes,

As we turn and fix our eyes on Jesus, we look away from false cultural idols, breaking our gaze, which is what gives cultural idols their power. . . . Through faith in the work of Jesus, however, we are able to see what is possible for our lives and to embrace authentic beauty in the world. As we regard our bodies free from false expectations, they can become temples of God's Spirit. Personal adornment becomes an act of affirmation and not an act of self-loathing. As we see its cruelty, violating our bodies through cosmetic surgery, excessive dieting, and bod-mod becomes repulsive to us. . . . It allows us to look in the mirror without shame and to see others with new eyes. We will see beauty where we saw lack. We will see our naked faces reflecting the love of God. Because Jesus absorbs our shame, we will no longer feel compelled to offer up our body to the pursuit of inauthentic beauty devoid of true justice. We can see beauty in unexpected places and faces and join Jesus in embracing the untouchable, the marginal, and the broken.

Finding the balance comes not so much in a list of dos and don'ts as in asking ourselves some deeper questions. *What behaviors come from body obsessions? What behaviors are the result of body neglect? How can I treat my body in ways that will point others to God? How can I make choices that model modesty? What things have become idols that need to be thrown out? Is there anything God may want me to fast from for a while? What behaviors could be ways of decorating my temple for the divine resident within me?* There may be more questions than answers, but as we wrestle with the Holy Spirit over these issues, we may find ourselves landing in a place of healthy balance.

SCRIPTURE TO MEMORIZE

Do you not know that your body is a temple of the Holy Spirit, who is in you, whom you have received from God? You are not your own; you were bought at a price. Therefore honor God with your body.
1 CORINTHIANS 6:19-20

QUESTIONS FOR DISCUSSION

1. What has God been teaching you about body obsessions and body neglect?

2. What would it look like to treat your body like a temple?

3. When it comes to modesty, how good are you at being a "secret keeper"? Tell each other ways that you see each other modeling modesty well. How about ways to improve?

4. In what ways do you need help in making your body a healthy and cared-for place for the Holy Spirit to reside?

5. Look over some of the questions in the final paragraph of the chapter. What sticks out to you the most? What might God be saying to you about reaching a healthy balance?

7 ✐ IS THERE MORE THAN MEETS THE EYE?

Beauty and Character

BEAUTY MAY BE SKIN DEEP,

BUT UGLY GOES CLEAR TO THE BONE.

✐ Redd Foxx

*Y*ears ago my husband and I took a job as houseparents on a university campus. We were to live in a house with forty-two women and take care of the building, grounds and meals. Our love for college students made us excited for the opportunity to live with them. But I have to admit, when we first moved in I was a little bit intimidated by the cute and very well groomed girls in the house. OK, so maybe I was extremely intimidated. However, it didn't take long for that to change. For sure it helped that many of the girls were very warm and friendly and fun to be with. But I stopped being so intimidated by their physical appearances once I met Dana and Lori.

These girls were both gorgeous by cultural standards. I'm sure that Victoria's Secret would have gladly included them in its catalog. The only thing more noticeable than their good looks was their vicious tongues. The two girls complained about absolutely everything. If it wasn't about the house, they were spewing venom about their classes, their lunch, even their friends. They were in a perpetual state of crabbiness, the way you might be if your little toe got run over by a bus every time you went outside. Their pretty faces were overshadowed by their ugly attitudes. It was like Helen Hunt said in *As Good As It Gets:* "When you first came into the restaurant, I thought you were handsome. But then you opened your mouth."

To be clear, I did grow to care deeply for Lori and Dana. The longer I lived in the house and learned about their lives, the more I understood what had contributed to their sour attitudes—their brokenness, their disappointments and their struggle to feel loved. I longed for them to be free from the pressure to look a certain way, and I wanted them to know Jesus and the joy he brings. But I learned a valuable lesson from these two girls. External appearance is ultimately not what makes a woman beautiful.

> *External appearance is ultimately not what makes a woman beautiful.*

INSIDE OUT

Inner beauty? I used to shrug off the concept. Inner beauty always seemed an ethereal concept that had nothing to do with real life. It was the kind of thing mentioned by great-grandmothers with knitting needles who still refer to underwear as "bloomers." Be nice. Be polite. Be good. Smile a lot. Oh, come on. In real life, it's the girls with killer good looks who get the attention. Nice girls get passed over. In a culture that rewards women's external features, the concept of inner beauty seems a bit like a trite Hallmark motto on a refrigerator magnet. "Beauty is like a watermelon. It's sweetest on the inside." Whatever. The last thing I want to feel like is a watermelon the next time I'm trying on jeans.

I've since discovered there really is a kind of beauty that has nothing to do with external appearance. Herein lies the most powerful form of beauty: the composition of our character. This is more than refrigerator-magnet beauty. It is not mustered up from good manners and positive thinking. This is the most striking beauty of all. It is a beauty that never fades or fails. It is a beauty so powerful that it overshadows any impression that external appearance can make. It is the beauty of our character when we're living for Jesus.

One of the best examples of this may be a woman named Esther. If anyone in the Bible has the reputation of being noted for her appearance, it's her. But a closer look at her story reveals that what really makes Esther beautiful is the character she exhibits when choosing to follow God's purposes.

We learn immediately that Esther was "lovely in form and features" (Esther 2:7). Before being brought before the king, she received a full year of beauty treatments. That's right: her own personal makeover, complete with pedicure, personal chef, cardio instructor and a makeup artist to the stars. This girl must have been pretty hot, since she beat out all the other young women of the kingdom in King Xerxes' little beauty pageant. Her prize? The royal crown and a banquet in her honor.

But notice what really shines about Esther. It's not her rock-hard abs or her freshly bleached teeth. What stands out about Esther is her character. There are only four verses that make reference to Esther's incredible appearance. The remaining contents of the book's ten chapters paint the picture of her moral fiber. The main point of the story is how God uses her when she risks her life to stand against racial injustice. What is breathtaking about Esther is not her bust line and braids; it is her God-given courage, her commitment to justice, her love for mercy and righteousness, and her self-sacrificing service to others.

True, Esther's physical beauty was a good gift from the Lord. He used her appearance to put her in a strategic place of influence. But

Esther didn't derive her security from being pretty. She didn't hide behind it. Her value wasn't the sum total of her appearance. In the story of Esther, her physical beauty plays a role, but it fades into the distance as her character comes into view.

So many of us get this backwards. We think that our physicality is the reigning feature that communicates our beauty, and we get fixated on it. For years the only thing I remembered about Esther was that she became queen because she was pretty. I'm sure that if I had met Esther back then I would have been entirely too intimidated by her good looks to even speak to her. I would have then consumed myself with comparing my loathsome body to hers over a pint of Moose Tracks ice cream, pausing now and then to be disgusted by the wealth that gives her access to expensive skin creams and the latest exercise equipment. If I had written the book of Esther, nine chapters would have gone on about her appearance and the tenth would have ended with "Oh yeah, and she risked her life to save the Jews from mass genocide."

> ✐ But notice what really shines about Esther. It's not her rock-hard abs or her freshly bleached teeth.

Thankfully, God's view of physical beauty is drastically different. It's a good thing because God made it. But it's far from the main thing. First Samuel 16:7 says, "The LORD does not look at the things man looks at. Man looks at the outward appearance, but the LORD looks at the heart." Esther's heart truly overshadowed her appearance. It was the beauty of loving God and his purposes that made her stick out, that changed the course of history and that leaves a legacy for believers to emulate today.

In stark contrast stands the story of David's son Absalom (2 Samuel 14—18). As St. Augustine once said, "Beauty is indeed a good gift of God; but that the good may not think it a great good, God dispenses it even to the wicked." Absalom was just that, physically beautiful yet rebellious. We are told that "in all Israel there was not a man so highly praised for his handsome appearance as Absalom. From the top of his head to the sole of his foot there was no blemish in him" (2 Samuel 14:25). But this guy became so full of bitterness and rage that he hired a hit man to kill his own brother. He spent several years running from the law and hiding out. He then gathered a posse (who wouldn't follow such a gorgeous guy?) to overthrow the throne of his father, David. Talk about a dysfunctional family. In the end Absalom was violently killed. What stands out about Absalom? Certainly not his good looks. Again, a person's character will eventually overshadow any kind of impression his or her physical body can make.

> "Beauty is indeed a good gift of God; but that the good may not think it a great good, God dispenses it even to the wicked."
>
> St. Augustine

It doesn't take long to identify real-life Esthers and Absaloms. The physical appearance of one of the most beautiful women I know pales in comparison to the beauty that comes from her soul. Don't get me wrong. She is attractive on the outside. Anita is one of those women who look great with any hairstyle—her eyes always sparkling and a smile that could stop traffic.

But to be honest, I don't really pay much attention to Anita's appearance. That's because her character is exquisite. She oozes grace and encouragement and passion for Jesus. She gets angry at injustice and weeps over sin. She will blow your socks off with a challenge from God's Word, and her joy is contagious. She is warm and deep and funny and gifted. It doesn't really matter what Anita wears or how she cuts her hair. She is breathtakingly I-want-to-be-just-like-that beautiful.

Who are the Esthers and Absaloms that I know?
What are the character traits I've seen
in others that I want to possess?

❧

LOOKING BEAUTIFUL OR BEING BEAUTIFUL

Author Debra Evans writes in her book *Beauty and the Best*, "The notion that looking beautiful equates to being beautiful . . . is false from a biblical point of view." God tells us in his Word that it isn't our wardrobe that will really turn heads. It's a spirit that reflects Jesus.

"Thanks be to God, who always leads us in triumphal procession in Christ and through us spreads everywhere the fragrance of the knowledge of him. For we are to God the aroma of Christ among those who are being saved and those who are perishing" (2 Corinthians 2:14-15).

Did you catch that picture? When Roman military leaders won a battle, they were often granted a victory parade through the streets of Rome. As a Roman citizen, the apostle Paul used this metaphor to make a point about life. It's as though the crowds have gathered, as on Madison Avenue on Thanksgiving Day. As we journey through life, God leads us down the middle of the masses, and what strikes them is not something they can see. The air is filling with an unforgettable aroma. God is spreading the sweet fragrance of his kingdom—the fragrance of new life, of broken things made whole, of cravings satisfied, of lost being found, of chained ones set free, of weeping turned to dancing. This is the mark of a true follower of Jesus. We

❧ "The notion that looking beautiful equates to being beautiful . . . is false from a biblical point of view."

DEBRA EVANS

fill the earth with his irresistible perfume, inviting others to worship him.

How do I respond to the thought that God wants to use me to spread the fragrance of his kingdom?

How quickly we forget that the most beautiful thing about us may be something we can't actually see. Paul Brand is a surgeon who has given his life and talents to God's kingdom by offering reconstructive surgery to the disabled and working to find treatments for leprosy. He writes,

> The beautiful, the strong, the politically powerful, and the rich do not easily represent God's image. Rather, His spirit shines most brightly through the frailty of the weak, the impotence of the poor, the deformity of the hunchback. Even as bodies are broken, His image can grow brighter. . . . I do not say that a Miss Universe or a handsome Olympian can never show forth the love and power of God, but I do believe that such a person is, in some ways, at a disadvantage. Talent, a pleasing physical appearance, and the adulation of crowds tend to shove aside the qualities of humility and love that Christ demands of those who would bear His image.

Every morning when I get dressed, I can spend a great deal of energy being concerned with what I put on. Who will I see today? Do I need to look trendy, or can I get by with a pair of sweats? Are these jeans too tight? Does this shirt flatter my chest without crossing the line of modesty? Are these the right shoes, the right jewelry, the right underwear? You never know, I might just run into a Hollywood agent who will take one glance at me and think, *Wow, she looks so great that I must make her famous and rich and successful. Good thing she isn't wearing raggedy sweatpants.* OK, so maybe I won't meet someone from

Hollywood, but at least the gas station attendant will like me better.

But I'm learning that it's much greater gain to redirect that energy to *dressing myself with Christ*. Paul understood this well. Over and over again he encourages believers to dress themselves with things of Jesus. His letter to the Ephesians describes *putting on* spiritual armor—belts and hats and shoes made not from fine Italian leather but from God's gifts and empowerment (Ephesians 6:11-18). Eugene Peterson's *The Message* renders Paul's words to Timothy this way: "I want women to get in there with the men in humility before God, not primping before a mirror or chasing the latest fashions but *doing something beautiful before God and becoming beautiful doing it*"(1 Timothy 2:9-10, emphasis added). It seems Paul is trying to tell us to dress ourselves with the attitudes and actions that indicate we love Jesus. This is about being beautiful, not just looking beautiful.

GETTING DRESSED

Dressing ourselves with Christ isn't just an abstract metaphor. It requires intentional action. In the same way that I establish daily routines to take care of my physical body, like bathing, exercising and putting on clothes, there are regular habits that help me "put on" the things of Jesus. These are the actions that will grow me in character beauty.

Am I spending regular time with God—reading the Bible, listening to what he might be teaching me, journaling my conversations with him, pouring out my heart, putting into action what I am learning? Becoming more like Jesus isn't a magical transformation that happens without our intentional involvement. Committing ourselves to the habit of daily quiet time opens a way for God to grow in us striking beauty traits like humility, integrity, perseverance and love for others.

Am I building relationships with those who need to know God's love—the lost, the hurting, the marginalized, the broken, the oppressed? As we give ourselves to others, speaking truthfully about the good news of Jesus, serving in practical ways and learning from them, God frees us from self-absorption and grows in us the beauty of selfless love, servanthood and compassion. As Isaiah 52:7 says, "How *beautiful* on the mountains are the feet of those who bring good news, who proclaim peace, who bring good tidings, who proclaim salvation, who say to Zion, 'Your God reigns!'"

Am I using every part of my life to build God's kingdom? Do I see my time as his—my money, my career, my relationships, my possessions, my family, my goals, all tools for God's purposes in the world? Owning and embracing deep, eternal-life purpose is a character trait that is extremely attractive. Making choices that grow us in generosity, faith and justice makes us beautiful.

My friend Ling has taught me much about character beauty. As a young woman, Ling felt "normal" levels of body insecurity. She would compare herself to others and didn't like feeling "average" about her appearance. But God taught her that he wanted to grow a deeper beauty in her that would be breathtaking, if only she would be intentional about pursuing it.

Ling recalls, "God began to show me that I needed to develop a character marked by humility. It seemed to come up all the time: in my quiet times, in sermons at church, in the retreats I'd attend, in the things people prayed for me. God was saying, 'It's time to really pursue this.'" So she decided to be deliberate about it. She studied anything she could find in Scripture about humility. She read books on it. She prayed for it. She looked for opportunities to apply it. No matter what situations came her way, Ling asked, *How do I respond humbly?* She intentionally devoted a season of her life to growth in humility. She muses, "As God molded my character, I realized that he was growing something beautiful, truly beautiful, in me. That was so much better than conventional beauty."

Audrey Hepburn was a cultural icon of elegance and beauty in her day. Yet even Hepburn understood the scintillating beauty that comes from one's character. When asked for beauty tips, she once said, "For attractive lips, speak words of kindness. For lovely eyes, seek out the good in people. For a slim figure, share your food with the hungry.

For beautiful hair, let a child run his or her fingers through it once a day. For poise, walk with the knowledge that you never walk alone."

Investing heavily in our appearance is futile anyway. Our bodies will not last. No matter how much anti-aging cream I use, my body will still age. No matter how much I fuss over my hair, it will still return to dust someday. Yet "we do not lose heart. Though outwardly we are wasting away, yet inwardly we are being renewed day by day. . . . So we fix our eyes not on what is seen, but on what is unseen. For what is seen is temporary, but what is unseen is eternal" (2 Corinthians 4:16, 18).

✍ Our bodies will not last. No matter how much anti-aging cream I use, my body will still age. No matter how much I fuss over my hair, it will still return to dust someday.

Does this mean I should ignore my body? Certainly not. But the real question is, what have I devoted myself to—what do I fix my eyes on? I can invest in something that will last. I can make sure that I am growing the beauty that comes from Jesus in me—things like purity, integrity, servanthood, love, kindness, compassion and conviction. I can spend myself on things that are eternal, things that grow God's kingdom, things like justice, evangelism, service, worship, helping others know Jesus better. These are the things worth my time and effort. These are the things that will ultimately create an unfading beauty in me.

These are also the things that will grow the family of God. The reality is that the more I invest in my physical appearance, the more others notice me. But the more I invest in God's purposes, growing in character beauty, the more others see Jesus in me. If I want to see others fall in love with Jesus and be part of God's kingdom, then I will pursue the beauty that points to him instead of simply emphasizing my physical traits.

How can I be intentional about pursuing character beauty?

THE GOOD, THE BAD AND THE BEAUTIFUL

After all this talk about inward beauty, you may be wondering if physical beauty is a bad thing. What about those of us who have physical features that our culture has deemed beautiful? Are we to feel guilty? Does God reject physical beauty? Should we? I don't think so, and let me explain why.

Where I live in the Midwest, there are not very many recreational options for someone looking to have some fun. A good time means making a trip to Super Wal-Mart, going to see a movie or watching the corn grow. Usually the movie wins out. When one is in desperate need, there's always the bowling alley on the nearby college campus. But just the thought of bowling makes my palms sweat. I'm a terrible bowler, and there is one reason for that: I overcompensate. If I bowl too far to the right, the next time I'm guaranteed to throw a gutter ball on the left. It makes me incredibly inconsistent. My score boxes suggest that I've got multiple personality disorder and I've let each character take a turn: 5, gutter, 3, gutter, strike, gutter, gutter, 8, spare, 6, 1, strike, gutter.

It seems to be our nature to overcompensate. If something turns sour, we abandon it altogether. Bad waitress experience? We decide never to return to that restaurant. Bad boyfriend experience? We conclude that the concept of dating is bad. You've probably heard the saying "Don't throw the baby out with the bathwater." I'm not sure why we still use the analogy, since these days there's no way a whole baby could fit down the tub drain. But the point is that just because our culture has wrongly elevated physical beauty as the highest attribute does not necessarily mean that physical beauty is bad. If beauty itself were bad, it would stand to reason that Scripture would speak of it that way.

Beauty is actually mentioned in the Bible more than I had ex-

pected: approximately a hundred references. There is quite a variety of good things that God's Word considers beautiful. Many of
them are inanimate objects, and their beauty is considered an asset:
houses, crowns, garments, ornaments, flocks, cities, clay vessels,
mountains, nature. Some beautiful things are people groups, like
the city of God or the nation of Israel. Sometimes it is the action of
believers, like bringing good news or pouring expensive perfume
on Jesus' feet. In each case the beauty of these things is admired,
evidence of a good God and his splendor. In Scripture, God affirms
beauty—all beauty, not just the lim-

Beauty is actually mentioned in the Bible more than I had expected: approximately a hundred references.

ited list of what our culture defines
as beautiful. Ecclesiastes 3:11 says,
"He has made everything beautiful
in its time."

Even God himself is called beautiful several times. In Psalm 27:4 the
writer proclaims, "One thing I ask of
the LORD, this is what I seek: . . . to
gaze upon the beauty of the LORD." If
God himself is called beautiful, then
the connotation of beauty must be positive. It's no wonder that we—
God's creatures—want to be considered beautiful. Beauty is a good
trait to possess. Maybe it's even evidence of being created in the image of God.

I wonder if that may be why the Bible also includes women's physical appearance among things considered beautiful. Sarai, Rebecca,
Rachel, Abigail, Bathsheba, Tamar, Abishag, Esther, Job's daughters,
Solomon's beloved—all are described as being very beautiful. There
is something very appropriate, even worshipful, about appreciating
the beauty that our Creator has made, whether physical or not.

But in our pursuit of beauty, we somehow manage to mess things
up. We have invented our own hierarchy for beauty, one that pre-
vents us from noticing the things God considers beautiful and ulti-

mately steals the admiration that should be lavished on the Creator instead of the created. I once read it put this way: "The case against beauty is idolatry—a worship of and trust in one's own beauty. . . . It is not beauty itself that is indicted in this vision; beauty itself is a gift conferred by God. What is condemned is the perversion of beauty in pride, self-absorption and self-worship."

Herein lies the pitfall for all of us, whether we fit the cultural standards of beauty or not. We can easily become worshipers of physical beauty and fall into pride. One type of pride is the puffed-up version. It says, "Compared to everyone else I come out on top. My appearance makes me better, and as a result I require praise. Affirm me. Affirm me." The other type of pride is actually self-loathing. It says, "Compared to everyone else, I come out on bottom. My appearance makes me worse, and as a result I am hungry for praise. Affirm me. Affirm me." Either way, we have placed ourselves at the center of attention instead of the One who created our body in the first place.

God despises our pride when we become worshipers of physical beauty, when our appearance becomes something we want others to praise. Isaiah wrote,

> The LORD says,
>   "The women of Zion are haughty,
> walking along with outstretched necks,
>   flirting with their eyes,
> tripping along with mincing steps,
> with ornaments jingling on their ankles.
> Therefore the Lord will bring sores on the heads of the
>   women of Zion;
>   the LORD will make their scalps bald."

In that day the Lord will snatch away their finery: the bangles and headbands and crescent necklaces, the earrings and bracelets and veils, the headdresses and ankle chains and sashes, the perfume bottles and charms, the signet rings and nose rings, the fine robes and the capes and cloaks, the purses and mirrors, and the linen garments and tiaras and shawls.

Instead of fragrance there will be a stench;
    instead of a sash, a rope;
instead of well-dressed hair, baldness;
    instead of fine clothing, sackcloth;
    instead of beauty, branding. (Isaiah 3:16-24)

Yikes! Baldness? Stench? God despises self-worship so much that he threatens to take away all the things that these women have trusted in.

Not long ago my parents announced that they were moving to a new home, and we went to help them pack up and clean out their house. I started in on a closet that was full of things that had been stashed away after my sister and I had moved out. It was a smorgasbord of memories: old ballet costumes, a graduation tassel, my sister's spoon collection. The best find by far was a small tattered and worn blanket, the kind that looks like long underwear with satin edging. It was my old security blanket.

There's a reason it's called a security blanket. These blankets start out with a practical purpose: to keep our tiny baby bodies warm. But we grow up with the blanket. It becomes like a bedtime friend. Familiar. Soft. Comforting. It bears with us through nightmares and flu season and monsters under the bed. If it were up to me, I would have had embroidered on my blanket, "It was the best of times, it was the worst of times." We even give our blankets nicknames like "binky," "wubby" or the ultra-creative "blankie." But long after our body grows large enough that the blanket isn't able to fully cover us, we still insist on sleeping with it. It makes us feel secure.

I obviously don't sleep with my blanket anymore. That's because I figured out the difference between a blanket that keeps me warm at night and a security blanket. True, both are blankets. But you reach a point of maturity when you recognize that it's unhealthy to become emotionally dependent on something, even a good thing. Growing up means being secure enough by yourself that you don't need a blanket to help you. A blanket can be just a blanket.

How is physical beauty like a security blanket for me?

Physical beauty, too, can be like a security blanket. God made our bodies purposefully to reflect the beauty of his creativity. But the moment we lose sight of the purpose of our physical beauty—to reflect the image of God—our beauty becomes something it was never intended to be. And in the end it isn't physical beauty that makes us most beautiful anyway. Just as we saw for Esther and Absalom, the true measuring stick of attractiveness is a life that models Christ. This is true for all of us, whether we seem to fit cultural beauty standards or not.

So at this point I'm left alone with the question, *What will be most important to me?* The difference between looking beautiful and being beautiful rests in whether it's more noticeable that I bear the image of Christ or that I bear the image of Tommy Hilfiger. The more I invest in my physical appearance, the more the world notices *me*, not Jesus in me. Will I devote myself to my own image so that the world will see *me*—polished, perfect, pleasing? Or will I be devoted to bearing the image of Jesus, so that the world sees past me and notices the One who is most beautiful of all?

What do I spend most of my energy on— reflecting Jesus or maintaining an acceptable appearance? What has God been saying to me about looking beautiful versus being beautiful?

SCRIPTURE TO MEMORIZE

Your beauty should not come from outward adornment, such as braided hair and the wearing of gold jewelry and fine clothes. Instead, it should be that of your inner self, the unfading beauty of a gentle and quiet spirit, which is of great worth in God's sight.
1 PETER 3:3-4

QUESTIONS FOR DISCUSSION

1. What have you been learning about looking beautiful versus being beautiful?

2. What are some character traits that make a woman beautiful?

3. Talk about the ways you see one another reflecting Jesus and how that makes each of you beautiful.

4. How can "dressing yourself with Jesus" become part of your daily beauty routine?

5. What connotation does physical beauty have to you? Good? Bad? Shallow? Ultimate? How does that affect the way you view your body?

6. How does your answer to question 5 compare to the way Scripture views beauty?

7. How has physical beauty been like a security blanket to you?

8 ✍ WHERE CAN I GET A SUPERNATURAL MAKEOVER?

Beauty and Freedom

ONE CAN NEVER CONSENT TO CREEP

WHEN ONE FEELS AN IMPULSE TO SOAR.

✍ *Helen Keller*

*A*nybody want to ski?"

I think those are my four favorite words during summer. I was only eleven when my family purchased a ski boat and some land that gave us use of a lake. When classes were over on the last day of school, we were like captive animals set free in the wilderness, driving over hills and through wooded farmland until we reached our oasis nestled in a valley of apple trees. The warm embrace of the sun, the thrill of the speeding boat, the rhythmic lullaby of waves, the cooler full of goodies (and cute boys at the beach)—who could blame us?

Soon after acquiring the boat, my dad taught me to water-ski. I caught on so fast that it wasn't long before I surpassed his skill level and earned the position of ski instructor for friends and visitors wanting to learn. Like an Olympic coach training athletes for the gold medal, I would spell out every last detail for my eager pupils: how to wait in the water, where to position the skis, which hand signals to use, how to balance and steer. But something was missing.

Then I figured it out. I had to warn them about "the moment."

There comes a time—after the "ready" signal, after the zoom of the engine, after the rush of swirling water—when every skier has a moment of decision. When the boat has thrust forward, a battle ensues between current and swimmer. For while the boat skims effortlessly atop the water, the waves refuse to give up the swimmer's body. The lake grasps frantically at appendages, trying to pull its victim back under. It's a nautical tug of war. Inevitably the swimmer wonders, *Maybe I should just let go.*

There it is. The moment of decision. The moment when it feels like the current will win. The moment when we doubt that we'll ever emerge above the waves. The moment when the rope feels like a two-ton weight in our hands. The moment we must decide to hold on even tighter than before.

For if we push through, the current gives up. Bursting through the waves, we emerge atop the water, free, empowered, glistening in the sun. And what follows is the reason I love to ski. It's like soaring on glass. The wind in my hair. The warm waves lapping at my feet. The speed feeding my adrenaline. Where else do we get to play and jump and fly at forty miles an hour?

Some of us may be experiencing "the moment" right now. We've been swimming in the currents of culture—currents that have lied to us about our bodies. We want to rise above the tide and taste the adventure of God's freedom. We've even signaled that we're ready to get going. But as the engine roars, we find ourselves in the heat of a battle. Will the currents of culture win out? Magazine ads, peer pressure, Hollywood images, internal voices, wounds from the past, comfortable habits—all try to pull us back into the water.

Hold on tighter than ever. God wants to help us burst through.

What is my greatest obstacle to living in body-image freedom?

FREEDOM IN INTIMACY

For every water-skier, the key to getting pulled out of the water is the rope. Why? Because the rope is the only link between swimmer and power source, a boat engine with the strength of hundreds of horses. Holding tight to the rope actually causes a transfer of power. The swimmer becomes a skier by borrowing the horsepower of the engine and using it to overcome the resistance of the water.

> We have a source of power even stronger than a few hundred horses.

The same is true for us. We have a source of power even stronger than a few hundred horses. He is the One who fathers the drops of dew, who brings forth the constellations in their seasons, who sends the lightning bolts on their way, who endows the heart with wisdom (adapted from Job 38:28-36). The most amazing part is that this very same God wants to know and love me! Hanging on tight to my connection with him gives me access to the same kind of power that raised Jesus from the dead.

I really turned a corner in dealing with my poor body image and learning to care for my body when I realized that I had been holding on to a rope, but it wasn't tied to the proper power source. My feelings about my body had reached an all-time low. I had been steadily gaining weight over several years, and my body was the largest it had ever been. Working with younger college students, I was reminded regularly that my body wouldn't fit into the cute clothes they were wearing. I was embarrassed and tried to hide my body in baggy clothing, hoping no one else would notice my ugly bulges. I knew I should probably do something about it, but it just felt too hard. I felt defeated, embarrassed, ashamed and disgusted with myself. I even remember dissolving into tears a few times.

During that time, a friend had found some success losing weight by joining a weight-loss program. So I thought maybe I would give it a try. I admit, at the time my motives weren't about making my body healthy. I really just thought that if I could lose weight, I might come closer to looking like the "ideal beauty," and then, for sure, I would find contentment. Thankfully God was aiming a bit higher than I was.

The program taught me to be mindful of how I nourished my body, and it encouraged regular exercise. So I started a routine of pushing a stroller on long walks. For a strong extrovert, spending significant portions of time without a conversation partner feels as fun as counting ticks on a monkey. And since my child was too young to hold a conversation beyond "What does the duck say?" I decided to converse with God in prayer.

> ✍ Food was my counselor, my antidepressant, my hobby, my companion, my comfort and my reward. . . . Now I couldn't turn to food, and it forced me to turn to God to meet those needs.

I was not expecting God to break through as he did. The first thing he did was to teach me that my spiritual habits had been just as unhealthy as my eating habits. While I was learning about nutrition—portion sizes and what kind of fuel my body really needs—I was also learning about my lifestyle. With a limited amount of food each day, I couldn't just eat mindlessly whenever I felt like it. This forced me to deal with the reasons I had been eating. I quickly realized that most of the time I hadn't been eating to fuel my body. I'd been turning to food to comfort me in times of stress, times of depression, times of boredom, times of procrastination and even times of joy. Food was my counselor, my antidepressant, my hobby, my companion, my comfort and my reward. Food had been sitting on a throne in my life that belonged to Jesus. But now I didn't have that option. I couldn't turn to food, and it forced me to turn to God to meet those needs. My prayer life took off.

It wasn't an easy transformation. But God was showing me that my unhealthy habits fed my unhealthy self-image. The first step was breaking my addiction to food and replacing it with an intimate dependence on the Lord.

Food isn't everyone's addiction of choice. Sometimes we fill up on guys, or alcohol, or perfect grades, or new clothes. Some of us even are addicted to the feelings of control that come from restricting our diet, overexercising, or cutting or burning our body.

I will never forget the time when God used my two-year-old to reveal another unhealthy addiction I had. It was bedtime, and we were almost done with the evening ritual. Teeth were brushed, pajamas on. Family members were kissed. Now we were reading a story before bed. It was a little board book called *The Good Shepherd*, the kind with a little flap to lift on each page. As the story goes, a shepherd boy has a bunch of sheep, and his job is to watch over them. But tragedy strikes—one little lamb gets lost. I reached over and carefully lifted the flap, reading the cliffhanger question underneath: "Where did she go?" Without missing a beat, my daughter looked up at me and with conviction answered, "Shopping!"

I laughed. *It must be her female DNA shining through.* But her sweet little voice was deeply convicting. I get a thrill out of shopping. There is some kind of adrenaline rush that comes from spending money. I usually crave it when life isn't going so well.

I've become much more aware of the times when I have a forceful urge to eat or to shop. Then I have to stop myself and say, *What is really going on here? What am I running from? What feelings am I trying to numb? What is the condition of my soul right now?* Because chances are, I really need to spend time with God instead. Do I always choose well? I wish I did. I'm still a weak and sinful woman. But the times when I choose to go to God and deal with the issues in my life have provided some of the richest food my soul has ever tasted. And the biggest difference is in the minutes afterward. When I choose to eat or shop, I may escape for a moment, but my issues are waiting for me upon my return to reality, made worse by feelings of guilt about indulging. But when I turn to Jesus, he helps me capture my issues and surrender them to his good plans. We deal with them together. Second Corinthians 10:3-5 says, "For though we live in the world, we do not wage war as the world does. The weapons we fight with are not the weapons of the world. On the contrary, they have divine power to demolish strongholds. We demolish arguments and every pretension that sets itself up against the knowledge of God, and we take captive every thought to make it obedient to Christ."

When I have a forceful urge to eat or to shop, I have to stop myself and say, What is really going on here? What am I running from?

Making healthy choices for my body helped me to make healthy choices for my spirit. My body was reacting well to the disciplines of taking better care of it. Imagine that. I lost about forty pounds, and my energy level increased. But it was during my times of prayer that the greatest transformation took place.

As I spent more time talking with Jesus, turning to him to deal with needs that I had formerly medicated with food, God also began to speak to me about how I felt about my body. He whispered about how much he loved me. He spoke about how beautifully he had crafted me. He assured me of my great worth. He declared me a masterpiece made by the greatest Artist ever to have lived. The truths of Scripture were branded deep within me.

I believe God's Word is, as it promises, living and active. Reading and studying the truths about my body and my value as a woman can change me. But there is something about hearing it from God himself—when God says, "My child, *this* is true for *you*"—that deepens the transformation. Whatever has previously blocked the truth from traveling from my head to my heart melts away at the voice of the Lord.

I was learning to take better care of my body. I was learning to turn to God instead of addictions like food or shopping. I was learning to love the body that God chose for me. It was all the result of connecting to God, the only source of power that could pull me out of this mess.

> *What might God want to say to me about intimacy with him?*
> *What things have I been turning to instead of God?*

FREEDOM IN CHOOSING

There is a second kind of freedom that causes change. It is the freedom of recognizing our choices. Things turned a corner for Olivia when she discovered it.

My friend Olivia struggled to love her body for most of her life. Her insecurity heightened when she spent time around her coworkers. She felt intense pressure to look exactly right at meetings and on business trips. Her clothes had to be perfectly flattering and trendy, her hair done just right. Puffy eyes or an untimely zit would have meant complete self-conscious embarrassment. Better to have a root canal than to be caught looking subpar.

The Lord had been speaking to Olivia about her unhealthy body image. She knew she needed to change the way she felt about herself. But how?

One weekend she was away at a conference with her coworkers. It was the last morning, and she was completely frazzled. Her alarm clock declared mutiny and failed to go off. She'd lost about thirty minutes of primping time. With no time to style her hair, she was just going to have to throw it up in a ponytail. She had spilled coffee on herself yesterday, and the only outfit left was definitely not one of her favorites.

Olivia glanced at her reflection in the bathroom mirror, almost afraid to see what would be looking back at her. She blurted out to God, "Why do I have to care so much about what they think of me?"

Olivia was a bit surprised at God's response: "You don't."

"What do you mean, I don't?" she snapped.

"It really is your choice. You can choose whose opinion matters to you," God tenderly replied. "Today, choose mine. I love you. And I think you're exquisite."

It was then that Olivia realized she really did have a choice in the matter. God reminded her of a passage in the Bible she'd been reading just the other day.

> Count yourselves dead to sin but alive to God in Christ Jesus. Therefore do not let sin reign in your mortal body so that you obey its evil desires. Do not offer the parts of your body to sin, as instruments of wickedness, but rather offer yourselves to God, as those who have been brought from death to life; and offer the parts of your body to him as instruments of righteousness. For sin shall not be your master, because you are not under law, but under grace. (Romans 6:11-14)

Notice the words used here. Do not *let* sin reign . . . *offer* the parts of your body . . . *offer* yourselves to God . . . *offer* the parts of your body . . . sin shall not be your *master.* These words imply action. They imply intentional choice. They imply an empowered will. Scripture says that we are in control of our own bodies. We are in control over how we think, what we believe and how we act in response. Paul taught the believers in Rome that in everything we have a choice. We either offer ourselves to sinful things or to righteous things. It's that simple.

It may seem a little unbelievable that we could choose once and for all to never be swayed again by others' opinions about our appearance. Rather, our choices come daily, one at a time. We make choices to give our body to sinful habits, sinful thinking, sinful desires. Or we make choices to give our body to godly habits, true thinking and selfless desires. It's one or the other, and we have the choice.

Olivia began to realize it was sin to value others' opinion of her over God's. It was sin to reject the body God graciously made for her. It was sin to crave the praise of other people. And she had a choice in the matter.

Olivia realized that day that she may not be able to control what other people think of her, but she can control whose opinion matters to her. She had always been able to do that with other things. Once a co-worker had said emphatically that the only fun thing to do on weekends was to get plastered. Had Olivia accepted that opinion without reservation? Of course not. Olivia knew that it wasn't true, that her life with Jesus offered more joy and laughter than an empty beer bottle. So she had dismissed her friend's opinion in favor of what she knew to be divinely true. Why couldn't she do that now?

> ✍ Our choices come daily, one at a time. We make choices to give our body to sinful habits, sinful thinking, sinful desires. Or we make choices to give our body to godly habits, true thinking and selfless desires.

Olivia pulled out a little yellow Post-it pad and scribbled down a few words that would become part of her morning ritual each day. She couldn't wait to get home and hang it on her bathroom mirror. Every time she got dressed in the morning, she would read aloud the words written to another group of believers: "Am I now trying to win the approval of men, or of God? Or am I trying to please men? If I were still trying to please men, I would not be a servant of Christ" (Galatians 1:10).

There is freedom when we realize that we don't have to be ruled by the opinions of others. While we can't choose what they think of our appearance, we can choose our own response. In fact, believing we have no choice but to let others define our worth is actually a choice in itself to offer ourselves to sin. We can consciously choose to listen instead to a heavenly Father who is proud of his artwork. We can choose to be grateful for the gift of this body instead of grumbling about it. We can choose contentment with our appearance instead of coveting what other women have. We can choose freedom.

What might help me to choose to offer my body to God instead of being swayed by the opinions of other people?

ℐ♥

FREEDOM IN GOD'S KINGDOM

Louisa May Alcott, author of the classic *Little Women,* once said, "Love is a great beautifier." Sometimes the key to finding freedom from our struggles with the beauty culture is in discovering that we've been paying way too much attention to ourselves and not enough attention to loving others. The missing link to finding the freedom we desire sometimes comes in focusing on the things of God's kingdom—the things that are bigger than we are, the things God desires to build in the world.

In his words to the nation of Israel, the prophet Isaiah suggests that our involvement in God's purposes will actually have a deeply transformational effect on us:

> Is not this the kind of fasting I have chosen:
> to loose the chains of injustice

> and untie the cords of the yoke,
> to set the oppressed free
> and break every yoke?
> Is it not to share your food with the hungry
> and to provide the poor wanderer with shelter—
> when you see the naked, to clothe him,
> and not to turn away from your own flesh and blood?
> Then your light will break forth like the dawn,
> and *your healing will quickly appear;*
> then your righteousness will go before you,
> and the glory of the LORD will be your rear guard.
> (Isaiah 58:6-8)

Tyra can't remember a time in her life when her appearance wasn't a pressure. In a family of five girls, beauty rituals were constantly a topic of discussion. As a college student, she was a bit apprehensive about taking a missions trip to Mongolia. She knew that life there would be very different. The team leader had been very specific about packing. Only a few pieces of modest clothing. No curling irons. No hair dryers. He insisted they weren't needed.

Tyra was a bit self-conscious at first. What would her teammates think of her if she couldn't do her hair every day? But it didn't take long before her concerns faded into the background as other issues took center stage. She and her teammates were building deep community. They were praying for the lost and looking for opportunities to share the gospel. They were serving the poor and living with families that had nearly nothing. God was teaching Tyra much about his love for the world and his plan to bring good news and restoration.

> ✍ Our involvement in God's purposes will actually have a deeply transformational effect on us.

She had been warned about reverse culture shock upon returning home. But Tyra hadn't realized how much her feelings about her appearance had changed during her month overseas. Coming home, she saw with new eyes what mattered in the scheme of eternity. Tyra still felt some pressure to blend in with the beauty culture, but she felt renewed by the taste of freedom she'd had. Immersing herself in God's purposes for the world had given her a reprieve from focusing so much on herself.

Some of us have spent so much of ourselves—our money, our conversations, our thoughts—being concerned about physical appearances, things that will not last anyway. What we really need to do is begin spending ourselves on purposes bigger than ourselves. I don't mean we should stuff our issues in a shoebox and pretend they aren't there. But as God reveals new truths about our body, our worth and his good plans for us, maybe our response should be to pray and then get up and love our neighbor. There is life and joy found in living out God's purposes in the world. Being actively involved in building God's eternal kingdom somehow shrinks our body-image issues into perspective and can get our mind off ourselves.

The surprising part is that, just as Isaiah suggests, God may even bring healing to the very thing we've chosen to take our mind off. Jesus is an amazing physician. The crowds who gathered around him knew this. In fact, Luke 6:19 recounts, "The people all tried to touch him, because power was coming from him and healing them all." Choosing to follow Jesus, to join him in building a new kingdom, is choosing to serve a divine doctor. Jesus loved to hang out with people who desperately needed to be healed, both physically and spiritually. Three of the four Gospels record these words in which he explained his ministry: "It is not the healthy who need a doctor, but the sick. I have not come to call the righteous, but sinners" (Mark 2:17). Making choices to focus our attention on loving others and building eternal things means that we enter into partnership with the Healer of our souls. We can pray that as we loose the chains of injustice, feed the hungry and clothe the naked, as we get up and love our neighbor, indeed "[our] healing will quickly appear" (Isaiah 58:8).

What is God asking me to do,
as part of building his kingdom and loving others,
that might put my body issues into eternal perspective?

𝒵❤

FREEDOM IN COMMUNITY

"Does this make me look fat?" she asked while modeling a new dress.

Her boyfriend looked like a deer in the headlights. *Not this subject. It's a no-win situation.* Not that the initial question was difficult to answer, but he knew where this was heading, and there was no way to maneuver through this minefield without somebody getting blown up. He stared into space, as if the question were the barrel of a loaded gun pointed at close range.

"You look fine," he mumbled as he quickly fled the scene.

Let's face it. Talking about body image with one another can be like walking on thin ice. So often our experience with other people, even people in God's family, is less than helpful when the topic comes up. Sometimes we're fishing for compliments. Sometimes we placate one another, wallowing together in our dysfunction. Sometimes we're afraid to say the wrong thing. Sometimes we're a target of harsh judgment. Sometimes we become the judgers. We joke. We avoid. We complain. We obsess. We criticize. Yuck. Who needs that?

I believe that within the context of community we can find real freedom. We are creatures who desire to belong. God made us that way. Belonging to a community that encourages us to be free of the lie of the beauty culture is powerful. It will take some hard work, of course, to develop a community like this.

1. *A healthy community has healthy conversation.* First, we must start with our own role in the community. The worst thing we can do is to

misunderstand the purpose of people who seek to be encouraging. They are not there to convince us that we are acceptable. That is God's job. It strains relationships when we expect someone else to do the work that only the Holy Spirit can do.

It's easy to put our friends in this awkward position. We so desperately want to know that we are accepted. So we start conversations in hopes that they can convince us that we are. Sometimes we even insult our own appearance, hoping that someone will swoop in and compliment us instead: "No, no. You have great eyes!" But this is not the kind of community that will bring freedom. It only feeds self-worship.

The same problem can show up in the form of sabotaging genuine compliments. Whether it's driven by shame or embarrassment or hunger for more compliments, we sometimes deny another person the opportunity to encourage us. In a healthy community we know how to receive compliments: by saying "Thank you" and audibly or silently crediting God with his good work in our life.

2. *A healthy community puts an end to judgmental or self-loathing talk*—whether it comes from our own mouths or others'. The community of believers in Ephesus was warned about this:

> Do not let any unwholesome talk come out of your mouths, but only what is helpful for building others up according to their needs, that it may benefit those who listen. And do not grieve the Holy Spirit of God, with whom you were sealed for the day of redemption. Get rid of all bitterness, rage and anger, brawling and slander, along with every form of malice. (Ephesians 4:29-31)

This means malicious talk about others but also about ourselves.

Getting rid of malicious talk is no simple task. It requires that we be on the watch for anything that attacks God's good design for our bodies. It requires that we speak the truth in love, even when we're afraid. It requires a conviction that humankind is so valuable to God that we refuse to let our words destroy like a vicious cancer.

It may also require getting rid of rituals that have been part of our relationships for years. Ever since I can remember, the girls in my family made a tradition out of watching the annual Miss America Pageant together. We would gather the necessary materials for our female bonding night: popcorn, chocolate, pillows, and a notebook and pen to keep track of the judges' scores. We would make a game of predicting the winner as early as possible.

🌿 In a healthy community we know how to receive compliments: by saying "Thank you" and audibly or silently crediting God with his good work in our life.

But as we got older, the tone of this event changed. It wasn't just a contest to watch. Half the fun came from criticizing the contestants. "Can you believe that dress?" "How in the world does anyone think that Oklahoma is prettier than Hawaii?" We were ruthless. I said things to that TV screen I wouldn't dream of saying to someone in person.

After a while I started to realize that this event, though nostalgic, was destroying my community with my family. It was allowing the currents of culture to distort the way we viewed those women *and* the way we viewed ourselves. The tradition had to end.

3. *A healthy community prays for one another.* Sometimes it never occurs to us to draw on the prayers of others to aid us in our deepest struggles. There are far too many groups of Christians that get together to pray but restrict themselves to completely impersonal requests. I call them "big toe" requests: we ask folks to pray for our test, our travels and the hangnail on our uncle's big toe.

Don't get me wrong. God cares deeply for the things that concern us and offers power to heal sickness. But often we squander opportunities to let other believers share in our spiritual struggles and intercede on our behalf.

A gifted pastor once told me, "When we confess to God, we find forgiveness. When we confess to one another, we find healing." James 5:16 reveals this very same truth: "Confess your sins to each other and pray for each other so that you may be healed. The prayer of a righteous man is powerful and effective." There is a power source of healing and freedom that we leave untapped when we don't ask others to pray for our body-image issues.

> ✐ Often we squander opportunities to let other believers share in our spiritual struggles and intercede on our behalf.

4. *A healthy community models what God has been teaching us about our bodies.* Talk about what God has been saying to you. Speak well of your body. Speak well of others. Say encouraging things about what makes them beautiful, physically as well as internally. Find partners in keeping your body healthy. Work out together. Shop together. Pray for each other. Be vulnerable. Make a commitment to one another that you will call attention to unhealthy talk. Create an atmosphere that says we don't always have to be dressed up or made up or gelled up to be accepted. Hang out with those who have trouble fitting in. Show them how God made them beautiful.

A community that treats one another this way is attractive. It's the kind of family the world longs to belong to. It's the kind of haven where the Holy Spirit is invited to bring healing. Lilian Calles Barger writes,

> I've often wondered: How many women with eating disorders are terminally lonely? How many eat their meager portions alone or gorge alone? How many women rushing to cosmetic surgery wouldn't bother if they felt they actually belonged to a community? How many casual campus sex hookups wouldn't

happen if young people felt valued by somebody somewhere? These sad things are not simply just personal problems; they are failures of the community.

I once read of a woman who understood what it means to be part of a community that understands that we are made beautiful by God and seeks to welcome others. When Karen left for college, she didn't know her life would change radically. Meeting a few Christian students, she felt drawn to their community because of the way they cared for her. Until then, Karen had been known as the girl with the moles. Dozens of them covered her face. She had been teased about it ever since she could remember. But these people were different. They loved her and let her know that she was special to God.

Years later, Karen decided that God was calling her to serve him in Africa. She had a gift of joy that was contagious, and she wanted others to know Jesus. One day, while walking through her new African village, she met a middle-aged man and began to talk with him.

He couldn't quit staring at her face. After a few minutes the man asked the translator to speak for him. "He says he wants to tell you that he's sorry about your face."

Karen's eyes beamed with confidence. "Oh don't be sorry!" she proclaimed. "Where I come from these moles are a sign of great beauty."

Part of building God's kingdom on earth means creating a community that is marked by a new culture. It is a culture unlike any other. Karen understood this. She had been transformed because her community had a different set of standards. Now God was using that community to change the world.

What can I do to help build a healthy community that encourages healthy body image?

℘

The point is not to look for an ideal community to join but to build life-giving communities with the people God has already placed around us. We can become channels of God's transforming power in each other's lives.

Suddenly the task isn't so daunting. God desires that we taste freedom. Not a false sense of security derived from imitating a twelve-inch plastic doll, but a deep security that bursts through the currents of the mainstream, creating a new culture and helping women to emerge free, empowered and glistening in the Son.

Overall, what has God done in my life as I have read this book?
Where will I go from here?

♪

SCRIPTURE TO MEMORIZE

Therefore, I urge you, [sisters], in view of God's mercy, to offer your bodies as living sacrifices, holy and pleasing to God—this is your spiritual act of worship. Do not conform any longer to the pattern of this world, but be transformed by the renewing of your mind.
ROMANS 12:1-2

QUESTIONS FOR DISCUSSION

1. In what ways are you experiencing "the moment"?

2. How would you describe your intimacy level with God? What things do you turn to instead of to him?

3. What practices or reminders help you choose to listen to God's opinion instead of the opinion of others?

4. How might acts of loving others and building God's kingdom help you take the focus off yourself?

5. What might it take to build an encouraging community around you?

6. How has your discussion group modeled an encouraging community for healthy body image? What has your group struggled with most?

7. Overall what has God done in your group? Where will you go from here?

A Note About Eating Disorders

Chances are that someone reading this book is struggling with an eating disorder. Very simply, this means any "disordered" relationship with food. Anorexia (denying the body food) and bulimia (eating—or sometimes overeating—and then purging the body of food) are the most widely known, but people can also have an eating disorder not otherwise specified (known as EDNOS). Conservative estimates tell us that five to ten million women are battling various types of eating disorders in the United States alone.

How do I know if I am one of them?

First of all, there is a definite difference between dieting and having an eating disorder. Although the term *dieting* can be used to describe dangerous eating habits, here I am simply referring to dieting as changing one's diet to make it more nutritious for the sake of improving your health. Dieting is about losing a reasonable amount of weight in a healthy way in order to do something beneficial for your body. Though it may be hidden behind the excuse of dieting, an eating disorder is based on the belief that food and eating (or lack of eating) are the key to changing one's entire life. Food becomes an enemy instead of a way to nourish the body.

Sometimes an eating disorder comes from a desire for negative attention. Sometimes its root is a desire to control our lives and emotions. Sometimes it is disgust for our body or ourselves. Sometimes it is a way of dealing with stress, pressure, pain, confusion, fear or anger. Whether we are aware of it or not, an eating disorder is usually a sign that we have felt out of control.

Still wondering? Your answers to a few questions from the National Eating Disorders Association can shed more light:

- Do you skip meals?

- Do you exercise so much that you are fatigued or have frequent injuries?

- Do you avoid eating meals or snacks when you're around other people?

- Do you constantly calculate numbers of fat grams or calories?

- Do you weigh yourself often and find yourself obsessed with the number on the scale?

- Do you exercise because you feel like you have to, not because you want to?

- Are you afraid of gaining weight?

- Do you ever feel out of control when you are eating?

- Do your eating patterns include extreme dieting, preferences for certain foods, ritualized behavior at mealtime, or secretive binging?

- Has weight loss, dieting, and/or control of food become one of your major concerns?

- Do you use diuretics, laxatives, or purging as a way of compensating for food you've eaten?

- Do you feel ashamed, disgusted, or guilty after eating?

The best way to discover an eating disorder is to honestly answer tough questions about ourselves. Maybe the most helpful questions are those listed above. Maybe we need to ask simply, *How do I feel about food?* Maybe we need to ask those closest to us to help us examine our life. Sometimes those around us are able to identify our unhealthy habits much more objectively than we can alone. No matter what, it is crucial that an eating disorder gets identified as such, because no matter how long it goes on—even if the behavior is on and off or just a few times a month—eating disorders actually destroy our body. We put ourselves in serious danger.

What can happen to our body? Malnutrition (which can lead to respiratory infections, kidney failure, blindness, heart attacks and death), dehydration (which can also lead to kidney failure, heart failure, seizures, brain damage and death), hyponatremia from drinking too much water (which can lead to fluid in the lungs, swelling in the brain, nausea, vomiting, confusion and death), muscle atrophy, paralysis, tearing of the esophagus, gastrointestinal bleeding, acid reflux, cancer, insomnia, swelling of the face or cheeks, hair loss, low blood pressure, high blood pressure, diabetes, ketoacidosis (high levels of acid in the blood, which can lead to coma or death), osteoporosis, arthritis, dental problems, liver failure, infertility, depression, suicide, cramping, diarrhea, ulcers, pancreatitis, fatigue and seizures. Oh, and did I mention—death.

If you have any suspicion that you may struggle with an eating disorder, the best way to care for yourself is to get help. Right now. You can talk to a friend, a pastor, a teacher, a counselor, a family member. You can tell them you need some help to find counseling. Search the Web for sites that will help. They are easy to find. Find a support group. Many hospitals offer them. Hunt down people who will commit themselves to pray until there is healthy progress. It would be a terrible tragedy to let embarrassment keep you from getting help, and ultimately cost you your life.

Sometimes we can know that our habits are unhealthy, dangerous even, but unless we are convinced that there is hope for change, we will remain slaves to our behaviors. I cannot emphasize this too much. *God is powerful enough.*

My friend Kylie would have never believed it. Her habits seemed to have a strength of their own. She knew that a seesaw between anorexic and bulimic tendencies was not a healthy way of dealing with her life. But each time she tried to fix it, her habits seemed to rebel and overpower her.

Finally she decided to bite the bullet and risk telling some friends who cared about her. They had seen warning signs, so they were relieved that Kylie was recognizing the problem, and immediately they began to pray fervently for her. They put together a list of helpful questions to ask regularly, and Kylie committed herself to answering honestly, even when she had messed up. And when that happened, her friends responded with prayer, with forgiveness, and also by talking through what thinking or actions had led to her mistake. Kylie's friends even set up a meal rotation, taking turns eating a meal with Kylie and spending thirty minutes with her afterward to make sure she didn't throw up. When Kylie spent several months in a residential treatment facility, they divided out shifts in a twenty-four-hour prayer chain, and they regularly sent her encouraging notes.

The Lord honored their prayers and commitment to one another. Kylie eventually found freedom from the habits that had mastered her. And she learned how to run to God when the same pressures and temptations returned.

God is powerful enough. He healed a woman who had been bleeding for twelve years. He brought dead kids back to life. He has turned the sea to dry land and flung open locked prison doors. He changes lives radically every day.

He can help you navigate your way to freedom. He really wants to. After all, you are his precious daughter. You're worth it. You are his masterpiece.

For more information about finding help or diagnosing an eating disorder, check out these websites:

• Something Fishy <www.something-fishy.org>

- Diets Don't Work <www.dietsdontwork.org>
- Focus on the Family <www.family.org>
- Remuda Ranch <www.remudaranch.org>
- American Association of Christian Counselors <www.aacc.net>

For further reading, check out these books:

Jantz, Gregory L. *Hope, Help and Healing for Eating Disorders.* New York: Random House, 1995.

Rhodes, Constance. *Life Inside the "Thin" Cage.* Colorado Springs, Colo.: Shaw Waterbrook, 2003.

Beyond Appearances: Parent's Guide to Eating Disorders (booklet). Colorado Springs, Colo.: Focus on the Family, 1999.

ᴢ᷃ NOTES

Chapter 1: The Lie We Buy

page 12 "It's been estimated that if Barbie": Elaine L. Pedersen and Nancy L. Markee, "Fashion Dolls: Representations of Ideals of Beauty," *Perpetual and Motor Skills* 73 (1991): 93-94.

page 13 "Barbie touches so many": Sharon Korbeck, *The Best of Barbie* (Iola, Wis.: Krause, 2001), p. 14. Korbeck cites this information from Gene Del Vecchio, *Creating Ever-Cool: A Marketer's Guide to a Kid's Heart* (Gretna, La.: Pelican Publishing, 1997).

page 14 "A recent survey found": B. J. Gallagher, *Everything I Need to Know I Learned from Other Women* (York Beach, Maine: Cohari, 2002), p. 109.

page 14 "Each year billions": Debra Evans, *Beauty and the Best* (Colorado Springs: Focus on the Family, 1993), p. 28.

page 15 "Magazine advertising revenue": U.S. Census Bureau, *Statistical Abstract of the U.S.: 2003* (Washington, D.C.: Government Printing Office, 2002), p. 794.

page 15 "Five out of six": Andrew Stephen, "Look Closely: Some People Are Not Real," *New Statesman,* March 4, 2002, p. 22.

page 15 "When asked about the dime": Nancy Etcoff, *Survival of the Prettiest: The Science of Beauty* (New York: Doubleday, 1999), pp. 44-45.

page 15 "Would you believe that 5": Dana Hudepohl, "How Much Would You Risk to Lose Weight?" *Glamour,* July 2002, p. 81.

page 16 "There's so much illusion": Judith Newman, "The Joys of Being Julianne," *Ladies Home Journal,* October 2004, p. 106.

page 16 "In the past three decades": Michael J. Devlin and April Zhu, "Body Image in the Balance," *Journal of the American Medical Association,* November 7, 2001, p. 2159.

page 17 "The average North American woman": Marnie Ko, "Blessed Are the Emaciated," *Report Newsmagazine,* October 8, 2001, p. 38.

page 18 "There's a reality to the way I look": Amy Wallace, "True Thighs," *More,* September 2002.

page 19 "Before the development of technologies": Naomi Wolf, *The Beauty Myth* (New York: HarperCollins, 2002), pp. 14-15.

page 19 "Most of our assumptions": Ibid.

page 21   "Some of my patients": Mindy Hermann, "Mothers, Daughters and Body Image," *Parenting,* April 2002, pp. 38-40.

page 22   "So saturated that": Beth Preminger, "The Jewish Nose and Plastic Surgery: Origins and Implications," *Journal of the American Medical Association,* November 7, 2001, p. 2161.

page 22   "My mother tells me": Alice Chung, "Anorexic," in *Yell-Oh Girls!* ed. Vickie Nam (New York: HarperCollins, 2001), p. 146.

Chapter 2: Was Eve a 36C?

page 31   "When I did my first": Kate Coyne, "Christie Weighs In," *Good Housekeeping,* July 2002, pp. 131-32.

pages 32-33 "formed in the": Judith Couchman, *The Woman Behind the Mirror* (Nashville: Broadman & Holman, 1997), p. 74.

page 38   "If we understand": Ibid., p. 75.

page 39   "The difference between": Lewis B. Smedes, *Shame and Grace* (New York: HarperCollins, 1993), p. 9.

page 40   "A pervasive sense": Merle Fossum, quoted in ibid., p. 3.

Chapter 3: When Beauty Becomes a Beast

pages 54-55 "Only about 20 percent": John T. Molloy, *Why Men Marry Some Women and Not Others* (New York: Warner, 2003), pp. 24-26.

page 56   "It may be": Loretta LaRoche, *Life Is Short—Wear Your Party Pants* (Carlsbad, Calif.: Hay House, 2003), pp. 72-73.

page 57   "I have stared": Monica Dixon, *Love the Body You Were Born With: A Ten-Step Workbook for Women* (New York: Berkley, 1996), p. 5.

pages 57-58 "Almost 20 percent": Ibid.

Chapter 4: Who's the Fairest of Them All?

page 62   "The rule was simple": Ingrid Banks, *Hair Matters: Beauty, Power and Black Women's Consciousness* (New York: New York University Press, 2000), p. 31.

pages 62-63 "a society wherein": Michael O. Emerson and Christian Smith, *Divided by Faith: Evangelical Religion and the Problem of Race in America* (New York: Oxford University Press, 2000), p. 7.

page 63   "In writings": Nancy Etcoff, *Survival of the Prettiest: The Science of Beauty* (New York: Doubleday, 1999), p. 42.

page 63   "We will not find": Ibid., pp. 42-43.

page 63   "Camper thought": Ibid., p. 43.

page 64   "By his standards": Ibid.

page 64   "House slaves": Ayana D. Byrd and Lori L. Tharps, *Hair Story: Untan-*

gling the Roots of Black Hair in America (New York: St. Martin's, 2001), p. 18.

page 64   "The most appalling": Etcoff, *Survival,* pp. 16-17.

page 65   "Our families, often": Sandra Guzman, *The Latina's Bible: The Nueva Latina's Guide to Love, Spirituality, Family and La Vida* (New York: Three Rivers, 2002), p. 53.

page 66   "I know Black girls": Dyann Logwood, "Hair Today, Gone Tomorrow: The Snarly Politics of Black Girls and Hair," posted on <www .AdiosBarbie.com>, 2002.

page 67   "In mainstream society": Ibid.

page 67   "When Afros came out": Banks, *Hair Matters,* p. 14.

page 68   "that the process": William H. Grier and Prince M. Cobbs, *Black Rage* (Eugene, Ore.: Wipf & Stock, 2000), pp. 42-43.

page 70   "To be *flaca*": Guzman, *Latina's Bible,* pp. 56-57.

pages 70-71   I grew up surrounded: Julia Wong, "Mirror, Mirror," in *Yell-Oh Girls,* ed. Vickie Nam (New York: HarperCollins, 2001), pp. 121-22.

page 71   Growing up among the blonde: Didi Gluck and Jenny Comita, "Black, Latino, Asian: A Very Special Make-Up Guide," *Marie Claire,* June 2004, p. 212.

page 72   We would get those eyes: Lois-Ann Yamanaka, "When Asian Eyes Are Smiling," in *Yell-Oh Girls,* ed. Vickie Nam (New York: HarperCollins, 2001), pp. 171-74. This article first appeared in the September 1997 issue of *Allure.*

page 74   Compared to a similar survey: Linda Villarosa, "Dangerous Eating," *Essence,* January 1994, p. 19, quoted in "Is the Face of Eating Disorders Only White and Middle Class?" <www.AdiosBarbie.com>, accessed 2002.

page 74   Another integrated study: Guzman, *Latina's Bible,* p. 58.

page 74   Even in Fiji: "TV Brings Eating Disorders to Fiji" <www. AdiosBarbie.com>, accessed July 3, 2002.

page 82   Since the birth of Hollywood: Guzman, *Latina's Bible,* p. 50.

Chapter 5: Who Are We Trying to Please?

page 90   "Not surprisingly, the": Nancy Etcoff, *Survival of the Prettiest: The Science of Beauty* (New York: Doubleday, 1999), pp. 44-45.

page 93   "Because we expect": Lilian Calles Barger, *Eve's Revenge: Women and a Spirituality of the Body* (Grand Rapids: Brazos, 2003), pp. 36-40.

pages 94-95   "The phrase *your desire*": Derek Kidner, *Genesis: An Introduction and Commentary,* Tyndale Old Testament Commentaries (Downers Grove, Ill.: InterVarsity Press, 1967), p. 71.

page 95   "Yearning to recover": Barger, *Eve's Revenge,* p. 139.

page 95   "As a result, a woman": Mary Ellen Ashcroft, *Temptations Women Face* (Downers Grove, Ill.: InterVarsity Press, 1991), pp. 116-17.

Chapter 6: Can I Still Keep My Favorite Lipstick?

page 102   "I would love": From *The Swan,* Fox network, program aired May 2004.

page 103   "A few critics": Michelle Green and Michael A. Lipton, "Beautiful Dreamers," *People,* June 7, 2004, pp. 59-63.

page 106   "In fact, obesity": Associated Press, "Global Anti-obesity Plan Gets Tentative OK," *Chicago Tribune,* May 22, 2004, sec. 1, p. 4.

page 109   "protective and overshadowing wings": Donald J. Wiseman, *1 and 2 Kings: An Introduction and Commentary* (Downers Grove, Ill.: InterVarsity Press, 1993), p 110.

page 109   "Possibly these symbolized": Ibid., p 110.

pages 111-12 "As soon as the weather": Amnita Ossom, "Trade That Spaghetti Strap for a T-Shirt," *Northern Star,* March 26, 2003, p. 11.

page 112   "According to the Gestalt": Dannah Gresh, *Secret Keeper: The Delicate Power of Modesty* (Chicago: Moody Press, 2002), p. 42. The diagram pictured is modified from a diagram found in ibid.

pages 112-13 "Again and again": Gresh, *Secret Keeper,* p. 21.

page 119   "Calls to ignore our": Karen Lee-Thorp and Cynthia Hicks, *Why Beauty Matters* (Colorado Springs: NavPress, 1997), p 94.

pages 120-21 "As we turn and fix": Lilian Calles Barger, *Eve's Revenge: Women and a Spirituality of the Body* (Grand Rapids: Brazos, 2003), pp. 172-73.

Chapter 7: Is There More Than Meets the Eye?

page 128   "The notion that looking": Debra Evans, *Beauty and the Best* (Colorado Springs: Focus on the Family, 1993), p. 138.

page 129   "The beautiful, the strong": Paul Brand and Philip Yancey, *In His Image* (Grand Rapids: Zondervan, 1984), pp. 40, 42, 46; quoted in ibid., pp. 165-66.

page 134   "Many of them are inanimate": Leland Ryken, James C. Wilhoit and Tremper Longman III, "Beauty," in *Dictionary of Biblical Imagery* (Downers Grove, Ill.: InterVarsity Press, 1998), pp. 82-83.

page 135   "The case against": Ibid., p. 85.

Chapter 8: Where Can I Get a Supernatural Makeover?

pages 154-55 "I've often wondered": Lilian Calles Barger, *Eve's Revenge: Women and a Spirituality of the Body* (Grand Rapids: Brazos, 2003), p. 192.

Appendix: A Note on Eating Disorders

pages 159-60   "Sometimes an eating disorder": Adapted from "Eating Disorder or Diet?" <www.something-fishy.org/whatarethey/edordiet.php>, accessed December 19, 2003.

page 160   "Do you skip": "What's Going On with Me?" <www.edap.org>, accessed December 19, 2003.

page 161   "Malnutrition": "Physical Dangers" <www.something-fishy.org/dangers/dangers.php>, accessed December 19, 2003.